ENGLISH COURSES

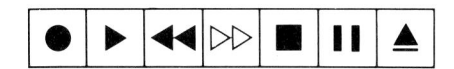

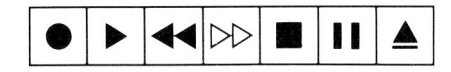

Fast Forward 2

Teacher's Book

VAL BLACK   MAGGY McNORTON
ANGI MALDEREZ   SUE PARKER

OXFORD UNIVERSITY PRESS

Oxford University Press, Walton Street, Oxford OX2 6DP

Oxford
New York Toronto Melbourne Auckland
Petaling Jaya Singapore Hong Kong Tokyo
Delhi Bombay Madras Calcutta Karachi
Nairobi Dar es Salaam Cape Town

and associated companies in
Berlin Ibadan

Oxford and Oxford English are trade marks
of Oxford University Press

ISBN 0 19 432305 6

© Oxford University Press 1987

First published 1988
Third impression 1992

All rights reserved. No part of this publication may be
reproduced, stored in a retrieval system, or transmitted,
in any form or by any means, electronic, mechanical,
photocopying, recording or otherwise, without the prior
permission of Oxford University Press

This book is sold subject to the condition that it shall
not, by way of trade or otherwise, be lent, re-sold, hired
out or otherwise circulated without the publisher's prior
consent in any form of binding or cover other than that
in which it is published and without a similar condition
including this condition being imposed on the
subsequent purchaser

Set in Helvetica light by VAP
Printed in Hong Kong

*The authors and publishers would like to thank the
copyright holders for their permission to reproduce the
following extracts in this book.*
The *Farmworker* and *Public Relations Executive* texts
(p. 73) by permission of the Sunday Telegraph
Magazine. The short story *True Love* by Isaac Asimov
(p. 94). Copyright © 1977 by the American Way from
The Complete Robot. Reprinted by permission of
Doubleday, a division of Bantam, Doubleday, Dell
Publishing Group, Inc.

*The publishers have been unable to trace and would be
pleased to hear from the copyright holders of the
extract from* The First Men *(p. 93).*

*The publishers would also like to thank the following for
their permission to reproduce photographs:*

Sally and Richard Greenhill; The Mansell Collection;
Network.

CONTENTS

Introduction	i
Classroom Organization	iv
Guide to Exercise Types	v
Scope and Sequence Chart	vii
Teacher's Notes and Lesson Plans	1
Optional Exercises	71

INTRODUCTION

Who is this course for?

Fast Forward 2 is designed for intermediate students who are interested in approaching the English language in a stimulating and interesting way. It is not suitable for anyone who believes that learning involves suffering. The authors have sought to bring pleasure and challenge to the learning process whilst keeping their materials based firmly on sound communicative principles. The course will be found particularly appropriate for learners on short intensive courses, where these materials were originally developed, but can be used to good effect with any group of committed adult learners.

By the intermediate stage the differences in learning styles and abilities will be very noticeable. While some students speak well, others are incoherent; some will write better than they speak; others will be systematic in their approach to learning, others will only concentrate on the skills that come most easily to them. In short an intermediate class is a mixed ability class and this can be an extremely difficult stage for both learner and teacher. Intermediate learners are often frustrated: frustrated because they know the structures but can't use them; frustrated because they can see no coherence or framework to the language; frustrated because they have reached the dreaded 'intermediate learning plateau' and it doesn't look as if they're ever going to get off. The sense of achievement of the early stages of language learning has gone and they have begun to realize just how much more there is to learn.

They express this frustration by asking for more grammar, more speaking, more listening or more vocabulary but then get angry with the teacher, the classbook and the course when none of these things solves their problem. In fact they actually need to tackle exercises that will activate the language they already have, to develop the confidence to experiment with that language, to accept that making mistakes is a stage on the road to speaking and writing correctly and to think about the language learning strategies they use to see whether these are the most effective for them.

With these needs in mind the 'Learning To Learn' sections have been included, not so much to tell learners how they should learn but to encourage them to think about how they learn and compare these strategies with those used by others in the group. Some students will need to tackle very few of the sections. To others the insight that other people learn differently from them is a useful revelation. Hopefully the more students realize how much they can help themselves to learn, the less dependent they will be on a teacher. This way forward is especially important for students on short courses, many of whom will want the means to go on learning after the course is over.

This Teacher's Book is designed to make life easier for the hard-pressed teacher. The authors are all practising teachers, well aware of the pressures that can build up from day to day and from one lesson to the next. With this in mind, they offer in this book everything a teacher will need to ease the burden of preparation – answers to selected exercises, guidance on appropriate techniques at every stage, supplementary materials, materials to photocopy and sample lesson plans for each unit. Everything, however, is offered on a 'take it or leave it basis' and it is fully expected that many teachers will choose their own way of handling the materials and will adapt them to suit the changing needs of their students.

What view of language underlies the course?

A look at the Lesson Plans at the beginning of each unit and the Scope and Sequence chart at the end of this introduction will reveal not just that the materials are communicatively based, but also that full account has been taken of all factors which contribute to successful communication: a confident command of structure, a good working vocabulary, sensitivity to the differing types of language appropriate in various situations, familiarity with a wide range of text types, a good balance between the skills of listening, reading, speaking and writing. There is also an implicit admission that language is complex: there is no attempt to delude the learners with over-simplification or to 'baby' them with graded down material. Instead, the authors have elected to organize the course into units, each containing a manageable 'chunk' of new language to focus on. In particular, the materials reflect a clear awareness that adult learners bring a certain degree of linguistic experience to the learning of English, and that this experience can be used to good advantage.

What methodological principles underlie the course?

The keynote here is flexibility. In the firm belief that the 'How?' of teaching will differ according to circumstances, the authors have offered a 'learning package' which can be regarded more as a teaching resource than just a textbook.

It is perfectly possible to use the book as a traditional course, beginning at the beginning and working through to the end; indeed, many learners and teachers may be happy with such an approach, for the present order of the units and of the activities in each unit is the most obvious one, and arises from the authors' own classroom experience. It may, however, be equally valid, with a particular group, to start at another point in the book, and to base the teaching programme on learners' linguistic needs or thematic interests.

Thus an interest in the developing world, for example, could be followed up through Unit 5 and Review Unit 4. Work on 'sequencing' and 'link words' could be developed from Units 5, 6 and 8. Similarly, within a unit there are several possible points of entry. A practice exercise, for example, could be used as a convenient linguistic instrument on which to base the teaching of that unit. Exercises and activities can be used to meet the group's needs and the choice in each unit is wide. Alternatively, any unit could be presented in a more traditional way. Possible routes through the materials are many and varied, and the choice depends on the group. Ideally, the group, with the teacher, will control the materials and not vice versa, always remembering that the best resource for teaching material is often the students themselves.

A further belief underlies the materials: namely that the process of learning is in itself an enjoyable and fruitful activity, and that the product-orientation so normal in consumer societies is not appropriate to language learning. Teachers need to be aware of the constantly fluctuating priorities of their learners and the dynamics of their classes. They should offer frameworks within which learners can express themselves but which at the same time challenge them as mature adults. The clear task-focus of the materials emphasizes this concern with the process of learning. This in turn enables the teacher to set up scenarios which will enable learners to acquire language inside and outside the classroom as well as to learn in more formal situations.

Any process-orientated approach is bound to involve contact and co-operation between learners. If this contact is to have any meaningful communicative value, account must be taken of affective factors in the classroom.

An individual's sense of comfort and security within a group is a vital pre-requisite for successful learning. Many of the tasks in this course encourage positive contact between learners in groups and pairs. For many adult learners, the experience of belonging to a class community is at the same time exciting and unnerving: in fact, the success of the course may depend as much on the establishment of a feeling of well-being as on any of the formal lesson preparation undertaken by the teacher.

How are the learners' needs met in the course?

The handing over of a coursebook to a learner by a teacher is a symbolic act involving faith and trust: many learners are brought up to view a coursebook as a fount of knowledge, as a point of reference during and after a course. Many modern English language coursebooks fail to live up to this expectation and are usable only in class under the supervision of a teacher. Learners feel frustrated if they cannot revise from their books, and ultimately insulted (as mature adults) at having to rely on a teacher for interpretation of the book. The chances are that such books will be thrown away or forgotten after a course.

In this course, the authors aim to keep faith with the learner by providing, in addition to the Classbook, a Resource Book containing summaries of essential language points as well as extra practice exercises for learners to tackle out of class. In recognition of a need for grammatical and lexical consolidation in a course with a communicative basis, many of these exercises focus on structures or vocabulary development.

The inclusion of the Tapescript and Answer Key means that the students can, if they prefer, work on their own. As a further aid to learning, a review unit has been built into the Classbook after every three learning units to enable both learners and teacher to take stock of progress and to revise. By reference to these units learners will be able to see and measure their own progress, and will not have to rely solely on the teacher's judgement.

One important expectation which learners have a right to have of their coursebook is that it will not bore them. This book is characterized by a variety of approach which ensures that there is no rut-like pattern following on from one unit to the next. Each unit is introduced and developed in a way which seems appropriate to the subject matter, thus ensuring variety within the overall framework of the Scope and Sequence chart.

Finally there is an implicit recognition that not all learners move forward at the same pace, and that some are stronger in certain skills than others. The Resource Book contains exercises which can be used as extra material for faster learners and this Teacher's Book contains suggestions for further activity, as well as photocopiable extra material.

A glance at the range of exercises and activities in each unit will reveal a balance between 'closed' and 'open' tasks, and between traditional exercises and more innovative activities. This represents an acknowledgement that different learners learn in different ways and find different activities useful. The aim is to provide something for everyone: thus the convergent thinker will probably prefer the 'closed' type of task, whilst the divergent thinker will find more to challenge her or him in open-ended activities.

How does all this affect me as a teacher?

The flexibility and variety that has been built into the course means that the teacher will have to be adaptable in her/his own approach. There will be times when she/he will prefer to keep a low profile as learners work on a fluency exercise in groups or pairs; at other times there is a need for a more teacher-controlled approach. The more experienced teacher will make comparatively little reference to the teacher's notes; they are written to make course and lesson planning easier for her/his less experienced counterpart.

What does a unit contain?

The only really common factor is that each unit offers material for 1½–2 hours of classwork. The variety of approach mentioned above means that each unit is different from the last one.

New language points are presented in each unit, but in different ways. Sometimes a text is used, sometimes a dialogue, sometimes the emphasis is on visuals, sometimes on a communicative task.

Each unit offers a balance of exercise and activity types to appeal to the different kinds of learner mentioned above. One learner may prefer a test plus exercises type of approach as it is fairly familiar; another may be happy to be stimulated to produce new language directly at the start of a unit.

There are a wide variety of listening passages including some which are authentic or adapted authentic and will therefore prove challenging. It may be advisable for the students to look at the exercises first, before listening, to provide clues as to what to listen for. Providing students with a copy of the tapescript may also be necessary for some groups. Emphasize however that the important point is always to understand the information relevant to the task and not every word. Exposure to authentic listening is important as early as possible to allow students to 'panic' in the safety of the classroom and therefore be better prepared for real life situations.

This Teacher's Book provides quick and easy reference to linguistic progressions. Each unit contains important 'nuts and bolts' information:

1 aims and objectives
2 materials and aids needed
3 identification of possible alternative entry points
4 notes on cultural content
5 notes on each stage in the unit
6 answers to selected exercises
7 instructions for the optional exercises

The book also contains suggested Lesson Plans for each unit, and, as an appendix, a series of photocopiable exercises.

Val Black
Maggy McNorton
Angi Malderez
Sue Parker

CLASSROOM ORGANIZATION

In case teachers are unfamiliar with some of the classroom activities suggested in this book, here is a brief summary of possible classroom organization.
(Notice the abbreviations: these are used throughout the book.)

1 Whole class activities (WC)

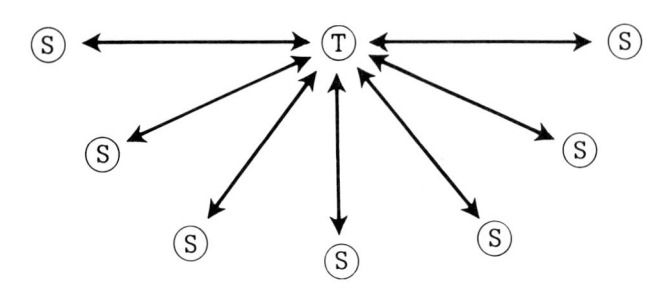

The teacher is in front of the students and talks to them either as a group or individually.

2 Group work (GW)

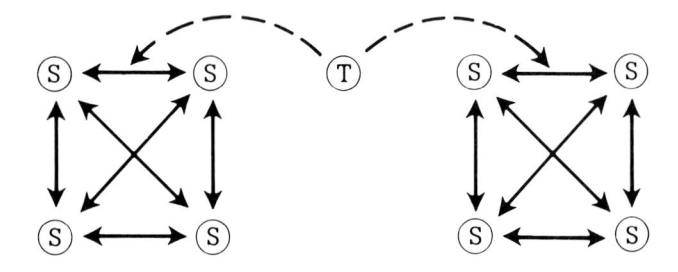

The class divides into groups of up to four or five. The teacher moves behind the groups and monitors.

3 Melée (M)

Students move around the classroom to obtain information or complete a task.

4 Pair work (PW)

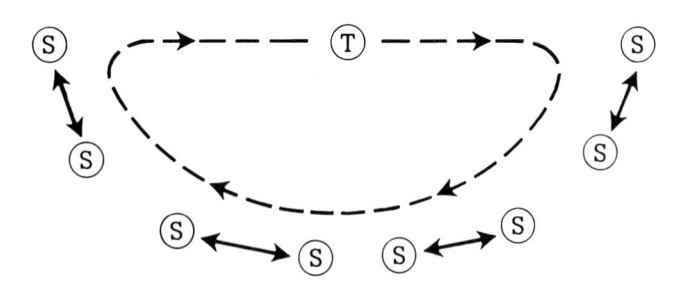

The teacher moves around from pair to pair, correcting or listening as appropriate. Students can stay in the same pairs or change for different activities.

5 Half/Half (HH)

The class divides into As and Bs. Each group prepares for the activity. The students then sort themselves out into pairs, one A with one B. The teacher monitors the conversations in the same way as for ordinary pairs. If time permits, students can redivide into different pairs, as many times as appropriate, but always ensuring that each pair comprises one A and one B.

6 Discussion (D)

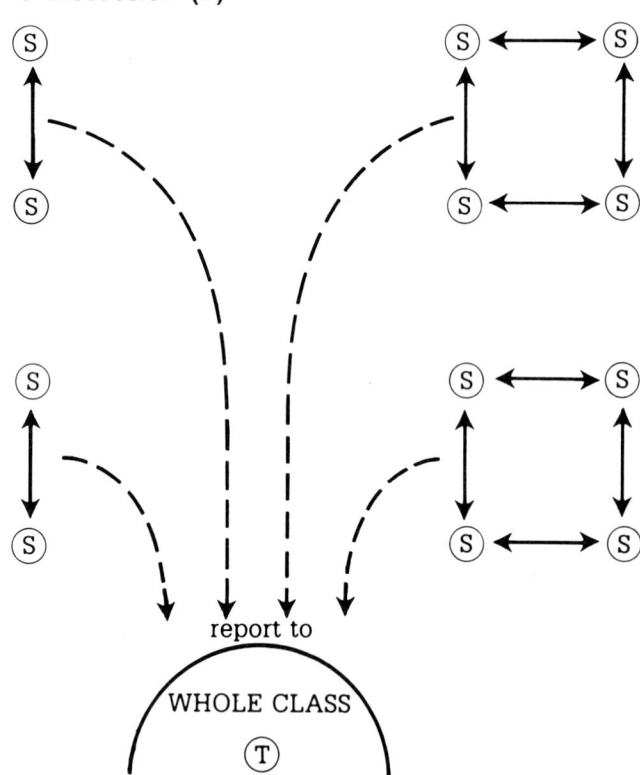

The class divides into pairs or groups, which then report the results of their discussion to the whole class. The teacher should monitor the pairs and groups and chair the whole class report-back. Alternatively one of the students may chair the report-back.

7 Roleplay (RP)

The students are given individual cards telling them the role they are to play. Give them time to read the card, so that they fully understand it.

The teacher explains new words and helps students to think themselves into the role. Then the teacher stays at the back of the class, listens and comments at the end.

8 Individual activities (I)

Students read, write, listen, etc. on their own, possibly as preparation for later work in pairs, groups or as a whole class.

GUIDE TO EXERCISE TYPES

Teachers using this book may find it useful to know what we mean by certain labels to exercises and activities. Here is a brief glossary which may be of interest and help to any teacher wishing to supplement these materials with exercises of her/his own.

Exercise Type	Classroom Organization	Description
Chaining	WC	Breaking down sounds in an utterance into small units to practise intonation, e.g. Excuse me . . . . Excuse me, can you tell me . . . . Excuse me, can you tell me where the station is, please?
Connected prose	I	
Crosswords	I	
Describe and draw	I, PW, GW	Drawing from information given by partner or teacher.
Dictionary work	I	
Discourse	I	Speaking in a linked pattern of discourse.
Chart	PW	
Creative writing	I, GW	Writing for content, not form, for process, not product.
Discussion	All except I	
Filling in forms	I	
Flow chart	I	Completing a drawing to show how particular systems connect with each other, e.g. sequences.
Focus listening	WC, I	Listening for a particular purpose, e.g. to find out where one of the speakers comes from (Review Unit 2, D).
Games	All except I	Anything with rules and/or a task to perform.
Gap filling	I	Inserting missing words into a text.
Grading	I	Self-evaluation of learning progress.
Information gap	All except I	Student A is the knower and Student B the seeker of information which is exchanged.
Information search	All	Extracting/looking for specific information.
Highlighting	I, PW	Underlining or extracting information from a written text.
Jigsaw	I, PW, GW	Unscrambling information to produce an ordered text.
Labelling	I	Naming parts of a diagram.
Language chart	I	Focusing on a language point, by means of boxes.
Linking	WC, I	Using linkers (joining words) to join sentences, e.g. 'but'.
Matching	I	Seeing a relationship between two pieces of information, e.g. vocabulary to pictures, structure to structure, ideas to ideas.
Maze reading	I, GW	Reading that entails decision making at intervals, the result of which determines the next section of text to be read, and so on to a more or less swift/satisfactory end.
Note-making	I, PW	Extracting information from a text in order to make personal notes, give opinions, etc., moving beyond the text.
Note-taking	I. PW, GW	Extracting specific information from a text and writing it down.

continued on next page

Exercise Type	Classroom Organization	Description
Pronunciation/intonation	WC, I, PW	Focusing on pronunciation/intonation by means of repetition, chaining, etc.
Questionnaire	I, PW, GW, M	Filling in answers to (written) questions.
Ranking	WC, I, PW, GW, D	Assembling information into a specified order.
Repetition	WC, I, PW	Repeating a model (see also chaining).
Roleplay/simulation	All except I	Students are given a new identity or a specific situation with which or in which to interact.
Summary	I, GW	Finding a title for a text, making a précis or retelling a story.
Thematic extension	All	Exercise to give further thematic information, rather than language information.
Thematic input	All	Exercise to introduce theme rather than language structure.
Transfer (referential)	WC, I, PW, GW	Following a model pattern, e.g. substitution in a model dialogue.
Vocabulary chart	WC, I, PW, GW	Completing a chart which shows the relationship between words belonging to similar or different lexical sets.
Vocabulary sets/sorting	WC, I, PW, GW	Putting mixed lists of words into the same word families.

SCOPE AND SEQUENCE CHART

Page	Unit	Communicative Functions	Topics and Vocabulary	Language Focus
2	Introductory Unit	Introductions	Getting to know each other Leisure Work	Present Simple Question forms Relative clauses: who Gerund/Infinitive
7	1	Asking for and giving directions Asking for information Saying where places are Describing places	Edinburgh Tourist information Towns	Prepositions
11	2	Offers and requests Arrangements Suggestions Hopes and plans	Food and drink Business conferences Entertainment	Modals: could/would/can Present Continuous for future arrangements Degrees of certainty
16	3	Complaining Apologizing Offering to put things right Accepting or refusing offers	Consumer problems Shopping	Present Perfect
20	**Review Unit 1** Part 1 Part 2	Revision Project	Multicultural Britain Eating out in Britain Unemployment Finding out about other countries	Revision
26	4	Describing things Describing people	Natural things Personality	Word order Relative clauses
31	5	Comparison Describing processes	Statistics Developing world Chewing gum	Passives Sequencing
36	6	Describing past actions and events	Customs and beliefs Myths	Past tenses Sequencing
40	**Review Unit 2** Part 1 Part 2	Revision Simulation	Britain: people, places and accents Dalelakemoor	Revision

Page	Unit	Communicative Functions	Topics and Vocabulary	Language Focus
46	7	Asking for and giving advice	Advice agencies Protecting your home 'Neighbourhood Watch'	Modals: should/ought to Gerund
51	8	Asking for and giving opinions Agreeing and disagreeing Expressing no opinion	Modern life Issues and causes	Link words Neither/Either
55	9	Expressing feelings Reacting	Gestures Romantic fiction	Adjective formation: ing/ed Question tags
61	**Review Unit 3** Part 1 Part 2	Revision Simulation	The British education system The Open University Kelapia	Revision
70	10	Expressing certainty and uncertainty Speculating about the future	Science fiction	1st and 2nd Conditionals
76	11	Deducing Speculating	Museum pieces Mysteries: The Bermuda Triangle	Modals: can/can't/may could/couldn't/ must/might
81	12	Regretting Wishing and hoping	A chapter of accidents Martin Luther King	3rd Conditional
86	**Review Unit 4** Part 1 Part 2	Revision Course review	Ethnic groups in Britain Carnivals and festivals Ways out and on	Revision

LESSON PLANS

Note: In the *Approximate Timing* column, each dot ● represents about five minutes classroom time. The square bracket { shows that the time given refers to two or more exercises. The round brackets indicate that the exercise is optional. The arrow > indicates the pattern of classroom organization in the exercise.

INTRODUCTORY UNIT

Approx. Timing	Section	Exercise Type	Classroom Organization
● ●	A1 Icebreaker/Diagnostic	Information Search	M
(● ●)	after A1 Optional exercise 'Who Am I?'	Information Search	M
● ●	A2 Practice/Diagnostic	Information gap	PW > GW
●	B1 Input	Ranking	I, PW, WC
	B2 Practice	Transfer	M
● ●	B3 Practice	Transfer	GW
●	B4 ▣Practice	Focus Listening	I, WC
● ●	C1 Input	Information Search	PW
● ●	C2 Practice	Questionnaire	I > M
● ● ●	D1 Reading	Information Search > information gap	I > PW
	D2 Practice	Discussion	PW, GW
●	D3 Practice	Discussion	GW
(● ● ●)	after D3 Optional exercise 'Earning a Living'	Questionnaire > Writing	I > PW > I PW > I
●	E Learning To Learn	Discussion	I > GW > WC

Communicative Functions
Introductions

Topics and Vocabulary
Getting to know each other
Leisure
Work

Language Focus
Present simple
Question forms
Relative clauses: who
Gerund/Infinitive

The main purpose of the unit is to create group cohesiveness and help students to get to know each other and their teacher.

Materials to photocopy: optional exercise 'Who Am I?'
additional job descriptions for Section D
optional exercise 'Earning A Living'

Materials to collect: none
Alternative Entry Points: any section; B4

A

BREAKING THE ICE

With a new group precede this activity with any name learning activity, e.g. the 'ball throwing game':
1 In a circle each person says his/her name as she throws the ball to someone else.
2 The receiver of the ball repeats the name of the person who has just thrown it.

1 Melée. Allow time for whole class reporting back. For further practice on defining relative clauses see Resource Book B1 and B2 for gerunds and infinitives.

Optional exercise

'Who am I?' Melée. Distribute photocopies of this exercise (page 72) and ask each student to fill one in. Collect the completed papers, shuffle them and redistribute them. Their task is to find the person who originally wrote on the paper. Tell the students to move around the room asking people about the facts written on the piece of paper they have.

Note any errors but do not interrupt the students. You may want to take part yourself. Stop the activity as soon as most people have found the right 'owners'.

This practises asking simple questions with:
'Do you like . . . ing?'
'Are you good/bad at . . . ing?'
'Have you ever . . . (done x)?'

2 Pair work > Group work. For further practice on question forms see Resource Book B3

B

INTRODUCTIONS

1 Individual or pair work or whole class. Introductory phrases are already ranked. Replies usually ranked as follows:

Informal Hi!
   Hello!
   Pleased to meet you.
   How do you do?
Formal I'm honoured to meet you.

NB Formality/informality are indicated by more than just words. Intonation, voice tone, body language, etc. are also important.

2 Melée. Check the appropriacy not only of the language but also of intonation, body language, etc. For further written practice on Introductions see Resource Book B4.

3 Group work

4 Whole class. Possibly extend by asking students to discuss what the speakers like, how they are standing, where they are, what they do, etc.

Conversation 1

Liz Sue! Sue!
Sue Hello, Liz! Long time no see!
Liz Yeah, I've been in Italy . . . [Oh!] . . . and erm . . . I'm getting married! [*laughter*].
Sue Really! Oh congratulations! And is this the lucky man?
Liz Yes, Sue, I'd like you to meet Carlo. Carlo, this is my old friend from school, Sue Cooper.
Sue It's very nice to meet you, Carlo.
Carlo I'm very pleased to meet you at last, Sue. I've heard a lot about you.
Sue Oh, [*laughter*] I hope it's good! [*laughter*].
Liz You'll have a lot of time to find out. Look, I'd like to invite you to the wedding.
Sue Oh!

Conversation 2

Kathy And do you know what he said then?
Man What? He sounds awful!
Kathy Well, he came in and . . .
Ms Blatchcombe Kathy, could you come in the office, please?
Kathy Oh . . . yes, Ms Blatchcombe.
Ms Blatchcombe Mr Porter, I'd like to introduce my personal assistant, Miss Kathy Jones.
Mr Porter Erm, how do you do, Miss Jones?
Kathy I'm pleased to meet you, Mr Porter.
Ms Blatchcombe Mr Porter is visiting us from the office in New York, Kathy, and I'd like you to show him around.
Kathy Yes, of course, Ms Blatchcombe. Erm, would you like to come with me, Mr Porter?
Mr Porter It'll be my pleasure, Miss Jones, or erm, may I call you Kathy?
Kathy Please do.

Conversation 3

Chairman Ladies and gentleman, [*coughs*] erm ladies and gentlemen, could I have your attention, please? [*coughs*] Thank you. Erm in order to celebrate the centenary of the Lakeside Bee-keepers Association we have one of the most famous experts in the field to speak to you today. It's my proud duty to present Lord Clarence Chapman. [*applause*]
Lord Clarence Thank you, Mr Chairman. Thank you, ladies and gentlemen. I'm very honoured to be invited to speak to such a knowledgeable audience on the occasion of their centenary. . . . The Lakeside Bee-keepers Association. . . .

C

TALKING ABOUT LEISURE

1 Pair work

2 Individual > Melée. Allow students sufficient time to discover common interests.

1 and **2** above could form the basis of a class project, perhaps for a later class magazine. Students could find out about facilities in their local area and write up the information. They could also write their opinions of the facilities, interview some people connected with different leisure pursuits, take photos, etc.

D

ASKING ABOUT JOBS

1 Individual/pair work. See page 73 for Job Cards C and D. If these are used, students work in groups of four.

An alternative exercise if using all four job cards is to first divide students into four groups. Each group works on one card and fills in the appropriate column. Redivide students into groups of four (one market gardener, one lorry driver, etc. in each group) to ask each other questions to complete the chart.

NB If you feel the reading passages are too difficult for your students or the time is too short you could ask the students to discuss their own jobs. Passages can be used at a later date as a review or homework exercise.

2 Pair work/Group work

3 Group work. For further job vocabulary see Resource Book B1 and E.

Optional exercise
'Earning a Living'. Pair work. Questionnaire for photocopying on page 74.

E

LEARNING TO LEARN

This section not only allows students to define their own personal goals for the course but also encourages a greater awareness and tolerance of other group members' goals. As an extension students can write down their own goals for the course and discuss their individual mini-goal for the first week and how they are going to achieve it. For example they could introduce themselves to as many people as possible or find an English book to read or learn ten phrasal verbs, or whatever they feel is appropriate for them. It is useful to ask students to report back, either in pairs or small groups each week on whether they achieved the goal. Students can then set further mini-goals. The activity helps students to assess the progress they are making as well as making them aware of their own responsibility in the learning process.

	Job A	Job B	Job C	Job D
Wages/Salary	£2,000 a year	£6,000–£7,000 a year	£346 gross a month £4,152 a year	£21,300 + perks
Hours	9 a.m.–5 p.m. 5½ days a week	40 hrs basic 50–60 hrs normal	40 hrs often longer	35 hrs often longer
Holiday	a fortnight	4 weeks	3 weeks	4 weeks
Qualifications	none	HGV class 1 licence	none	English degree from Oxford
Travel to work	—	by scooter	drives	drives
Length of journey	—	—	5 miles	30–40 minutes
Start work	9 a.m.	varies	8 a.m.	—
Finish work	5 p.m.	varies	6 p.m.	—
Like	her own boss	you are your own 'gaffer' on the road	variety in farming, countryside open air	variety, meet people, stimulating
Dislike	dirty low earnings	away at night tiring job	never know when you will get home	difficult to 'switch off'

UNIT 1

Approx. Timing	Section	Exercise Type	Classroom Organization
●	A1 Input	Chart	I, PW
●	A2 Practice	Transfer	PW
●	A3 Practice or	Transfer	PW
(● ●)	Optional exercise 'Discovering the Sights'	Reading > Information Search	I, PW
● ●	B1 Input	Information Search	PW
●	B2 Practice	Role Play	HH
●	B3 Practice	Role Play	HH
●	B4 Practice	Discussion	WC
● ●	C1 Vocabulary work	Labelling/Information Gap	I > PW
●	C2 Practice	Transfer	PW, GW
● ●	C3 Practice	Discussion	GW
●	D1 Thematic Input	Discussion	WC, GW
● ●	D2 Cultural Input	Discussion	WC, GW
(● ● ●)	Optional exercise 'Places in Britain' cards	Game	M
● ●	E Learning To Learn	Discussion	I > GW

Communicative Functions
Asking for and giving directions
Asking for information
Saying where places are
Describing places

Topics and Vocabulary
Edinburgh
Tourist information
Towns

Language Focus
Prepositions

The purpose of this unit is to make students aware of places of interest in the town where they are studying and to give them the language to get there.

Materials to photocopy: optional exercise 'Discovering the Sights' for A3
optional exercise 'Places in Britain' D2

Materials to collect: Tourist information for B. Maps of the town you are in.

Alternative Entry Points: any section

A

FINDING YOUR WAY AROUND

1 Individual or pair work. Possible acceptable alternatives:

| Excuse me, | could you tell me the way
could you tell me how to get
is this the (right) way
how do I get from here | to George Street, please? |
| | where is
am I right for | George Street, please? |

would you mind telling me where George Street is, please?

I'm looking for George Street. Can you help me, please?

| I'm afraid | I don't know.
I haven't a clue.
I haven't the faintest idea.
I've no idea.
I can't help you.
I can't tell you. | I don't live here either.
I'm a tourist too. |

2 Pair work

3 Pair work. If revision work is necessary you can use the following language chart either on the board or as a photocopied handout:

| Certainly
Yes of course | you go straight | down here
along there |

| until (you get to) the | traffic lights
museum | and take the | first road
second turning |

| on | the right
your left | and it's | on the corner.
in front of you.
next to the bank.
opposite the park.
on your left/right. |

Alternatively use maps of the town you are studying in, listing the main places of interest and alter A3 accordingly. For further practice on prepositions of place see Resource Book B1 and B2.

Optional exercise
Reading 'Discovering the Sights' for photocopying page 75. Answers: Individual or pair work.

1 John Knox's House	(4)	**6** The Zoo	(30)
2 The Castle	(1)	**7** Canongate Tolbooth	(11)
3 National Library of Scotland	(20)	**8** St Giles' Cathedral	(2)
4 Parliament House	(3)	**9** Hillend Ski Centre	(26)
5 Palace of Holyroodhouse	(5)	**10** Scott Monument	(6)

B
TOWN AND AROUND

1 Pair work. Skim-reading practice. The students need to have enough time to find the main pieces of information but not so much that they start trying to understand every word.

2 Half half. Extend the chart as necessary. Encourage the 'tourists' to go to as many 'information offices' as possible.

3 Half half. Again encourage as much 'visiting' as possible.

4 Whole class discussion. For further practice of time prepositions see Resource Book B3.

C
TOWNS – REAL AND IMAGINARY

1 Individual > pair work. Encourage the students to keep their drawings hidden from their partners.

2 Pair work, group work

3 Group work

D
PLACES IN BRITAIN

1 Whole class, group work

2 Whole class, group work. Answers:
1 Loch Ness
2 Ben Nevis
3 Aberdeen
4 Edinburgh
5 The Lake District
6 York
7 The Peak District
8 Snowdon
9 The Cotswolds
10 Cardiff
11 Exmoor
12 Stonehenge
13 The Norfolk Broads
14 The Giant's Causeway
15 Belfast

Alternatively use the optional place cards in the exercise below.

Optional exercise
'Places in Britain' page 76. Each student has one place card and identifies the town or area on the map on page 10. Collect in the cards. Melée. Students move around the class asking and listening to other students describe the town or area they have read about until everyone can identify all the places on the map.

E
LEARNING TO LEARN

Again this is awareness-raising in the interpersonal sense. Research would seem to suggest that:

1 Apart from phonological considerations, the older a person is the better for language learning.
2 This is partly true, however it depends on how meaningful the language was when originally learnt. Using a language in a meaningful way does help 'fix' it.
3 As students learn a language they should be able to express their own personality through it but as any language is deeply rooted in its culture they may find new dimensions to themselves too.
4 Everyone has a gift for languages – everyone has a mother tongue! It is true, however, that some people find it easier than others, for example, to imitate the sounds of the language or recognize its grammatical patterns. Motivation is also an important factor.
5 You can learn a language out of the classroom, but it may be more difficult without a teacher to communicate with.
6 Yes, but it is more effective if new words/structures are fitted into an existing framework, rather than trying to memorize them in isolation, e.g. traditional vocabulary lists.

UNIT 2

Approx. Timing	Section	Exercise Type	Classroom Organization
●	A1 Input	Focus Listening	I, WC
● ●	A2 Practice	Transfer	I, PW
	A3 Practice	Role Play	GW
(● ●)	Optional exercise 'Becoming a Picture'	Role Play	GW
●	B1 Input	Focus Listening	I, WC
●	B2 Practice	Transfer	I, PW
● ●	B3 Practice	Game	M
●	C1 Input/Practice	Transfer	PW, GW
●	C2 Practice	Transfer	PW, GW
●	D1 Input	Focus Listening	I>WC
● ●	D2 Input	Focus Listening/ Information Search	I>WC
	D3 Input	Focus Listening/Gap Fill	I>WC
●	D4 Practice	Discussion	GW
(● ●)	Optional exercise 'Role cards'	Game	GW
● ● ●	E1 Input	Focus Listening	I>WC
	E2 Input	Focus Listening/Gap Filling	I>WC
	E3 Practice	Note Taking/Discussion	I>GW, WC
	E4 Practice	Discussion/Role Play	PW
● ●	F Learning To Learn	Discussion	GW>WC

Communicative Functions
Offers and requests
Arrangements
Suggestions
Hopes and plans

Topics and Vocabulary
Food and drink
Business conferences
Entertainment

Language Focus
Modals: could/would/can
Present Continuous for future arrangements
Degrees of certainty

This unit concentrates on revising and extending 'survival' language, including small talk in a social situation.

Materials to photocopy: optional exercise 'Role cards' for D4
optional exercise 'Becoming a Picture' for A3

Materials to collect: random selection of pictures of people as optional extra/alternative to 'Becoming a Picture'

Alternative Entry Point: F

A

THE FIRST EVENING

1 🔊 Individual or whole class. Answers: boss – Anne; employee – John; friend – Sue; business associate – Robert. The formality/informality of the language and intonation should indicate the relationships.

Anne Well, this seems a good venue [Mm] Shall we go to the bar before dinner? . . .
John Erm, let me offer you a drink, Mrs Wright. What can I get you?
Anne Oh, just a tonic, thank you, John. And do call me Anne while we're away from the office.
John Erm, a tonic and a half of bitter, please.
Anne Oh look, there's Robert Jones from ICI. Good evening, Mr Jones.
John Evening, sir.
Robert Evening.
Anne Perhaps you'd like to join us for a drink?
Robert Ah, erm, Mrs . . . erm. Thank you, yes.
John Erm, what would you like, sir?
Robert Erm . . . scotch and soda, I think, please.
Anne Well, Mr Jones, it's ages since we met. . . .

Anne Sue! It's good to see you! Come over and meet everyone. But . . . oh, have a drink first. What'll it be?
Sue Anne! Oh, a . . . a gin and tonic, please. It must be three years since I saw you last, at least. Where was it? Brighton?

2 Individual/pair work. Possible answers:
1 Perhaps you'd like to join us for a drink/Let me offer you a drink?
2 Fancy a drink? How about a drink?
3 Come and have dinner?
4 Perhaps you'd like to join us for dinner?
5 Come and have a drink? Would you like a drink?

	Accept	**Refuse**
Formal	How kind of you? Thank you.	I'm sorry but I have a previous engagement.
	I'd love one. Thank you very much.	I'm so sorry. I'm afraid I can't.
	Lovely idea. Thank you.	I'd love to but . . .
Informal	Great! Thanks.	Sorry, another time.

NB Note that status is not the most important criteria for deciding appropriacy of language, e.g. your boss could also be a good friend, therefore informal language would be OK. Again remember intonation, voice tone and body language are important in these types of exchanges.

3 Group work. Possible preparation for this section is the roleplay 'Becoming a Picture' on page 78. Students choose from a large collection of pictures of people and 'imagine' themselves into that personality by use of prompt questions such as:

What's your name?
How old are you?
Where were you born?
What are your family like?
Where are they now?
Where do you live now?
What's you job?
How do you spend your time?
When have you been the most happy?
What has made you most proud?
What do you look like? – elegant, shabby, flamboyant, conservative, confident, anxious, ugly, defiant, withdrawn, plain . . . ?
What do you love, hate, admire, fear?
How do you walk, stand, sit, speak, meet others . . . ?

For further practice on invitations see Resource Book B1 and B2; for formal invitations see Resource Book B3.

B

AT DINNER

1 🔘 Individual or whole class. Anne is the vegetarian.

Anne I wonder if you could pass the menu, Mr Jones?
Robert Oh, I am sorry, of course! And erm, do call me Robert.
Anne Thank you. Oh dear, I don't know what to have ... I'm a vegetarian, you see. John, do you think you could catch the waiter's eye? Perhaps he can suggest something.
John Of course ... Erm ... Waiter!
Waiter Are you ready to order then, sir?
John Erm, I think we are, but, erm, Anne?
Anne Would it be possible for you to provide a vegetarian dish?
Waiter I'll see what I can do, madam.
Anne Oh, thank you. Well, for starters I'd like the melon. You too, I think, Sue. [Mm] And, John? ...
Sue Could you pass the water please, Anne? It's so hot [Mm] in here!
Anne Yes, isn't it? Shall we go out for a bit of fresh air?
John Oh, good idea!
Sue Would you mind waiting for me? I want to run up to my room for the conference programme. Then we can see what we're doing tomorrow.
Anne Of course! We'll meet you in the foyer.

Answers:
1 I wonder if you could ...
2 ... Waiter! (He caught his eye.)
3 Would it be possible for you to ... ?
4 Could you ... ?
5 Would you mind waiting ... ?
6 to get the conference programme

2 Individual or pairwork. Here appropriate language depends on the nature of the request as well as personality, relationships, etc. For possible answers, see the Language Summary in the Resource Book.

3 Melée. If your class have no ideas suggest such things as: sing your national anthem; do five press-ups; buy me a Coke at break-time. If necessary, revise the language for accepting and refusing requests:

Accepting	Refusing
With pleasure.	I'm sorry but that's impossible.
Certainly.	I'd rather not.
Of course.	I'm afraid I can't.
All right.	Sorry I can't.
OK.	

NB 'I suppose I could but ...' indicates reluctant acceptance. 'No, I can't.' is considered impolite.

For further practice in requests see Resource Book B4.

C

THE CONFERENCE PROGRAMME

1 Pair work or Group work

2 Pair work or group work

D

SATURDAY EVENING

1 🔘 Individual to whole class. They go for a sauna and a swim. Later they decide to go for a walk, and then to go out to dinner.

Sue Oh! I'm exhausted!
Anne Me too. But it's given me food for thought.
Barbara What's next?
Anne Oh, erm ... dinner! [Oh] But I'm really not hungry yet. How about having a sauna, anyone?
Sue Good idea! And a swim afterwards, all right?
Barbara Mm, that's fine by me. But not outdoors. I don't think it's quite warm enough for that! [*laughter*]
Sue Right!
Anne Well, shall we all meet at the sauna then in, say, ten minutes?
Barbara/Sue OK.

Sue So, what are we going to do now?
Anne Well, we could stay in and talk business, but I don't really fancy that. Or we could go and explore.
Barbara What about asking the receptionist what there is to do here?
Anne Fine. Ah, excuse me, I wonder if you could suggest what we could do in town this evening?
Receptionist Certainly, madam. Erm well, if you look over there at our display board, you'll see that there is a children's variety show on at one theatre, an amateur musical at another, [Mm] and a farce at the other. The local cinemas seem to be showing mainly children's films, but I've heard *Passage To India* is very good if you haven't already seen it. [Mm] You'll have to hurry though, because most programmes start at around 7.30.
Sue Well, thanks very much but erm, I don't feel like hurrying! Why don't we just walk along by the sea for a while?
Anne I agree, I don't feel like sitting and listening to anything more today. [Mm]

Barbara OK. Let's go.
Sue/Anne [Mm].

Barbara Oh, I do believe the sea air has given me an appetite. I'm hungry now!
Anne Hey, why don't we try and find that Moroccan restaurant the erm Mataam Marrakesh someone was telling us about?
Sue Mm, but I can't remember where it is!
Anne Then shall we phone, ask them where they are, and make a reservation?
Sue/Barbara OK. [Right]
Sue I've never had Moroccan food before, have you?
Barbara No, I haven't. Sounds fascinating. [Yeah]
Anne M... M.. Marra.. Ah, there we are. [*dials*] Ah, h, hello, Marrakesh Restaurant? Ah well, could I make a reservation for three for tonight, please? Yes. Oh erm, about eight o'clock? Yes, that's right. Eight o'clock for three. Oh, a, and can you tell me where you are exactly? Yes, ... I see ... Sorry, could you repeat that? Ah yes, I know. Thank you very much.

2 Answers:
1 talking business
2 Show Boat, Rod Hull and Emu, A Bedfull Of Foreigners.
3 musical – Show Boat; variety – Rod Hull and Emu; farce – A Bedfull Of Foreigners.
4 hurrying.
5 possible dialogue:

Anne Hello, Marrakesh Restaurant?
MR Yes, can I help you?
Anne Could I make a reservation for three tonight, please?
MR Yes, certainly. For three, you said?
Anne Yes.
MR What time?
Anne Oh, about 8 o'clock.
MR 8 o'clock?
Anne Yes, that's right, 8 o'clock for three, and can you tell me where you are exactly?
MR We're in Tor Hill about half way up the street.
Anne Yes, I see. Sorry, could you repeat that?
MR Tor Hill – it's at the top of the main shopping street. There's a big church opposite.
Anne Ah yes, I know. Thank you very much.

For further practice in telephone language see Resource Book B5.

3 See the tapescript in D1 above for the answers shown underlined.

4 Group work. For further practice of suggestions language see Resource Book B6

Optional exercise
Suggestions/role cards. Group work. See page 79. Organize students in groups of three and give each one one of the role cards. Ask them to make an arrangement for the weekend using the information from their cards to make suggestions and agree (or disagree) to them. One of the students will have to compromise. What do they decide to do?

E

HOPES AND PLANS

1 Individual to whole class. Answer: Yes, they've managed to re-establish their former friendship.

Sue Mm, that was delicious! I love the way they cook lamb.
Anne Yes, superb. I love the fresh herbs in the salads too. And my vegetable curry was perfect.
Sue Mm, I feel good! Well, Anne, you've done well since I last saw you. What are you planning to do now?
Anne Well, things are a little uncertain, as the company *might* be taken over by a multinational.
Sue What then?
Anne Well, in that case, I'll probably lose my job, but I'm hoping it won't come to that.
Sue You might be kept on.
Anne Yes, well, I'm intending to fight anyway. What about you?
Sue Well, if I'm not promoted soon, I'm thinking of changing jobs. [Mm] I'm getting a bit bored! Oh, work's all right really. It's my cottage I'm excited about really. I'm going to redecorate first, and then I'm planning to reorganize the garden. I can't wait!
Anne But what if you change jobs? You might have to move.
Sue Well, then I'll sell this one at a huge profit and buy a better one! [*laughter*]
Anne Ah well, one thing is sure – we're bound to meet again on the conference circuit sooner or later.
Sue We could try writing this time! What's your address?

2 See the tapescript in E1 for the answers shown underlined.

3 Individual to group work or whole class. See the Language Summary in the Resource Book.

4 Pair work. Emphasize that the students should imagine *themselves* as famous, not someone else.

F
LEARNING TO LEARN

1 Group work to whole class. This should encourage an awareness of the problem areas in the different skills for the members of the group.

2 There are many techniques for learning new words. F2 may give the students some new ideas and is an opportunity to discuss and encourage a positive attitude to the whole problem of selection and categorizing vocabulary which often worries students at this level.

UNIT 3

Approx. Timing	Section	Exercise Type	Classroom Organization
● ●	A1 Reading	Information Search	PW, GW
●	A2 Thematic Extension	Discussion	GW
● ●	A3 Reading > Writing	Information Search/(jigsaw)	GW, I,(>GW)
● ●	B1 Input	Focus Listening/Matching/Gap Fill	I>WC
●	B2 Practice	Transfer	PW
(● ● ●)	Optional exercise 'Talking Points'	Transfer	PW>WC
●	C1 Input	Focus Listening	I>WC
●	C2 Practice	Transfer	PW
●	C3 Practice	Discussion	PW, GW
● ●	D1 Input	Focus Listening	I>WC
	D2 Input	Focus Listening/Gap Fill	I>WC
● ● ●	D3 Practice	Role Play/Simulation	HH>M
● ●	E Learning To Learn	Discussion	GW

Communicative Functions
Complaining
Apologizing
Offering to put things right
Accepting or refusing offers

Topics and Vocabulary
Consumer problems
Shopping

Language Focus
Present Perfect

This unit revises and extends the language of apologizing and complaining, particularly in the context of shopping.

Materials to photocopy: replies to consumer letters in A1
optional exercise 'Talking Points' B2

Materials to collect: none

Alternative Entry Points: B, C, D, D3, E

A

CONSUMER PROBLEMS

1 Pair work, group work. The shop that acted legally was the one selling the duvet cover. The goods were not defective in any way.

2 Group work. Discussion.

3 Alternatives are to divide the class into three groups with each group working on one of the rules. Redivide into groups of three comprising one person from each original group to explain each rule. Or, divide the class into groups of three to six with each student/pair of students working on one rule so that they can explain it to the others in the group. Each group of three writes the replies. Class discussion to compare interpretations. For comparison use actual replies (printed below). For further practice in complaining, see Resource Book B1.

No. It may be 'company policy' to keep your money – but you don't have to accept it. You can insist on having your money back. If you did accept a credit note now, but didn't like any of their shoes, you'd have an even harder time trying to get your money back later. If you have a complaint, the Office of Fair Trading advises the following: stop using the item, tell the shop at once, take it back with the receipt (if possible), ask for the manager – and keep calm. Find out about your rights from the OFT's leaflet *How to put things right*, from Room 310C, Field House, Bream Buildings, London EC4A 1PR.

The short answer is yes. The shop is obliged to refund your money if the goods are not of 'merchantable quality' – if your duvet fell apart when you washed it, for instance, or if it wasn't 'as described' (say it was marked a king-size, but was only a standard double).

However, you are not entitled to any refund if you've just changed your mind. Some shops will offer money back or exchange goods, particularly if they're still wrapped and could be sold again, but they're not legally obliged to do so.

The other cases in which you wouldn't be entitled to a refund are if the faults are so obvious you should have seen them when you bought the goods; if the faults were pointed out to you, or if the shop told you the goods weren't suitable for what you wanted.

B

COMPLAINING AND APOLOGIZING

1 Individual to whole class. Answers: conversation 1 – picture 2; conversation 2 – picture 4; conversation 3 – picture 1; conversation 4 – picture 3. Check the notes made with the phrases underlined in the tapescript and/or the Language Summary in the Resource Book.

Conversation 1
Assistant Yes, sir, can I help you?
Customer I'm sorry but I bought this shirt yesterday and it hasn't got any buttons.
Assistant I'm very sorry, sir.

Conversation 2
Customer I'm sorry but I ordered a well-done steak. This one's rare.
Waiter I do apologize, madam. I'll get you another one immediately.

Conversation 3
Guest Well, I'm afraid I wanted a room with a view of the sea.
Manager All right, madam, I'll see what I can do. Let me see . . . Ah yes, the people in Room 129 are leaving tomorrow. I could let you have that room tomorrow [Erm] Would that be all right? [Well] I'm sorry about this.
Guest Yes, I suppose so. Thank you.

Conversation 4
Holidaymaker I'm sorry to have to complain, but I've just got back from a holiday you arranged for me, and the hotel was really awful! It was miles from the sea, the bedroom was filthy, the food was awful . . .
Agent Sorry about that. But it's not really our fault. The contract does say that the hotel accommodation is not our responsibility.
Holidaymaker That's just not good enough. I paid you a lot of money for that holiday . . .
Agent Well, perhaps we could give you a discount on your next holiday with us.
Holidaymaker No, that's quite unacceptable. I'll never book with you again . . .

2 Pair work. For more practice see Resource Book B2, B3 and B4. Additional practice on the Present Perfect can be found in Resource Book B5, B6 and B7. For Present Perfect/Simple Past comparison see below.

Optional exercise
'Talking Points' on page 79. Pair work. Give each student a copy to compare with information about his/her partner.

C

APOLOGIES

1 🔊 Individual to whole class. Answers: **1** Because his car broke down. **2** Because she hasn't rung the agency yet.

Mr Broughton Oh sorry I wasn't here for the sales meeting, Miss Bridges, erm, but my, my car broke down.
Miss Bridges Oh that's all right, Mr Broughton. We managed. But erm, I'm afraid I've got a confession to make too. [Oh] I haven't rung the agency yet about the extra sales staff. I am sorry.
Mr Broughton Ah erm, well erm, see if you can organize that this morning, will you?
Miss Bridges Oh, right.
Mr Broughton Thank you.

2 Pair work. Refer to the Language Summary in the Resource Book if necessary. Resource Book B2, B3 and B4 could also be used here.

3 Pair work, small groups. In addition, as an extension, the pairs can be changed with the student retelling either their own story or the story they've just heard to a new partner.

D

SHOPPING

1 🔊 Individual to whole class. Answers: **1** Kitchen Equipment **2** Coffee Bar **3** Food Hall **4** Clothes Department **5** Stationery **6** Knitwear

Conversation 1

Man Excuse me, [Sir?] I'm looking for a thing for opening wine bottles.
Assistant Erm, oh, a corkscrew, you mean. [Ah oui] Yes, they're on the counter beside the cutlery. [Merçi] Oh, good morning, Mr Broughton.

Conversation 2

Woman I think it's self-service here dear.
Man Erm . . . is it? Oh, oh yes, yes, perhaps you're right. Erm well, I'll go and get them. Erm (it's) white with sugar for you isn't it?
Woman Yes, oh, and if they've got a biscuit or something . . .
Man Right.
Assistant Morning, Mr Broughton.

Conversation 3

Woman Oh, excuse me, [Aye] I wonder if you could reach down that tin of beans for me, please?
Assistant Oh certainly, madam. Oh, Mr Broughton, we must talk to Food Display, those tins are much too high up.

Conversation 4

Woman Oh look, Jenny, that's nice! Oh it's in my size too. Erm . . . let's see. Oh yes, I like this! Have they got a 14, I wonder?
Assistant Can I help you at all? [Erm . . .] Lovely skirts, aren't they? They're new in. Would you like to try one on?
Woman Oh no, thanks, we're just looking.
Assistant Morning, Mr Broughton. Not much trade this morning, I'm afraid.

Conversation 5

Man Excuse me, erm yes, I'd (erm) like a pad of file paper.
Assistant Yes, sir.
Man Yes, and I a refill for my cartridge pen.
Assistant Ah, erm, like this one, sir? [Oh, yes . . .]
Man . . . Yes, those look right. How much is that?
Assistant Erm, that's erm, two pounds twenty please, sir. [Oh] Oh morning, Mr Broughton!
Man Yes, erm. [Two . . .] Oh, here you are.
Assistant Two pounds twenty. Erm, thank you.

Conversation 6

Woman I've been shopping in this store for 30 years, and I've never been so disappointed! I took it home! And just look at it! [Erm, yes.] I'd like to see the manager.
Assistant Certainly, madam. Oh, erm, Mr Broughton!
Mr Broughton Yes, Mrs Jones. Erm, is there a problem?
Woman I'm afraid I've got a complaint to make, as I was telling this young lady. I've been shopping in this store for over 30 years and I've never once been dissatisfied, but just look at this! It's shrunk, it wouldn't fit my grandson!
Mr Broughton Erm, yes, it has indeed shrunk! May I ask you if you followed [Hah! Hasn't it? Erm . . .] the washing instructions carefully?

2 Refer to the tapescript. The shopping theme could be elaborated by introducing other departments in a big store and/or comparison with small specialist shops, arcades, precincts, etc.

3 Use the picture of the market to set the scene for this activity. Half/Half. Divide the students into two groups, one group to be customers and the other to be stallholders. Both groups to discuss first the language they will need to use. Check that stallholders are selling a variety of goods (although it is more interesting if stallholders are sometimes competing) and ensure that students are confident before they embark on the actual roleplay.

E

LEARNING TO LEARN

Learning is a process that continues outside the classroom. This activity should help to make students more aware of this and also hopefully give them some new ideas to try out. Apart from the obvious advantages of wide reading (back of the Cornflakes packet, street signs, etc.), listening to the radio and watching the television, students may like to investigate such learning opportunities as eavesdropping on a stranger's conversation and trying to guess the relationship between the people; watching advertisements on TV with the sound turned down and then predicting the language that will come up when the advertisement next appears, etc.

REVIEW

UNIT 1

	Approx. Timing	Section	Exercise Type	Classroom Organization
Part 1 Language Review	• •	A1 Thematic Input	Discussion	PW, GW
	• •	A2 Vocabulary Work	Vocabulary Sets	I, PW, GW
	•	B1 Thematic Vocabulary	Vocabulary Sets	PW, GW
	• •	B2 Practice	Information Gap	PW
	• • •	B3 Practice/Writing	Discussion	GW
	• •	C1 Practice	Discussion	GW
	• •	C2 Reading	Matching	I, PW
	• •	C3 Practice	Role Play	GW
	• •	D Learning To Learn	Grading > Discussion	I > WC
Part 2 Project	• • •	**Stage 1** 1 Preparation	Discussion	WC > PW, GW
	• •	2 Library skills	Note Making	I, PW
	• •	3 Writing	Questionnaire	I, PW
	• • •	**Stage 2** Interview	Information Gap/Note Taking	PW
	• • •	**Stage 3** Reporting Back	Information Gap/Discussion	I, PW > WC

Topics and Vocabulary
Multicultural Britain
Eating out in Britain
Unemployment

Project:
Finding out about other countries

This unit provides additional practice and extension of the previous four units. Any of the Language Review Sections or the Resource Book could be used for diagnostic purposes or for extension of the units to which they refer. The Classbook extends functional practice whereas the Resource Book concentrates on further grammatical work.

Materials to photocopy: none
Materials to collect: (optional) encyclopaedias, atlases, etc. for Part 2
Alternative Entry Points: any section of the Language Review Section Project

PART ONE
LANGUAGE REVIEW

A
MULTICULTURAL BRITAIN

1 Pair work, group work. This exercise is intended to encourage discussion on the wide variety of people who live in Britain today.

2 Individual or pair work or group work. This topic offers endless opportunities for further extension work and helps to reinforce the rich variety of words in the English language.

Answers:
Shampoo – Hindi; bungalow – Hindi; chutney – Hindi; typhoon – Chinese; restaurant – French; doolally – English (British Army slang late *c.* 19-20); karate – Japanese; jodhpurs – from the town of that name in NW India; khaki – Urdu; admiral – Arabic; cafe – French; kiosk – Turkish.

B
EATING OUT IN BRITAIN

1 Pair work, group work. Curry – India; jambalaya – Louisiana, USA; lasagna – Italy; chop suey – China; kebabs – Iran.

2 Pair work. Revision of the language of directions.

3 Group work. The descriptions could be put on a board and added to as the students visit different restaurants during the course.

C
UNEMPLOYMENT

This exercise is intended to highlight some of the economic problems that Britain faces at the present time. Students should be encouraged to use the language of Suggestions, Hopes and Plans, Offers and Invitations.

1 Group work

2 Individual, pair work. Answers:
1 C
2 G
3 H
4 A
5 I
6 F
7 D
8 E
9 B

3 Group work. As students may find it difficult to 'get into' the roles it may be a good idea to allow all the students playing each role to prepare together. This is a good diagnostic exercise to assess how much of the language in the previous units needs to be revised.

D
LEARNING TO LEARN

Encourage the students to look at how they have assessed themselves and, for items not graded 'very well', ask them to decide if they want to know the item any better. If they do, suggest that they work out for themselves the best way of doing that. The Resource Book, if it has not already been used, may be useful here.

PART TWO
PROJECT

COMPARING COUNTRIES

This section is flexible. If only one lesson is available use Section 3 which gives practice in the use of question forms. However, if there is more time, Section 2 concentrates on library work and generally builds confidence in working outside the classroom.

Stage 1 Preparation

1 Try to encourage students to choose as interviewee, someone from a culturally very different country to their own.

2 This is a good opportunity to verify that students know how to use the school/town library, if necessary showing them round and doing preliminary library orientation work. Alternatively, if time or facilities prevent library visits, you will need atlases, encyclopaedias, etc. for reference in class.

3 Here is a chance to check accuracy of question formation and suggest individual remedial work as necessary.

Stage 2 The Interview

This can be organized in class time or given as 'home' (coffee break/lunch break) work.

Stage 3 The Report

This stage can be as elaborate or simple as time or enthusiasm dictate. From, for example, five minutes in small groups exchanging surprising/interesting facts about the researched country, to timetabled individual presentations/talks to the whole class with a follow-up whole class question/feedback session. The talks could be taped or videoed for subsequent language work, and in a cohesive, supportive group, feedback could include comments on fluency, audibility, interest of the delivery, content, etc. (The criteria should be made up and agreed by the whole group before the presentations begin.)

UNIT 4

Approx. Timing	Section	Exercise Type	Classroom Organization
● ●	A1 ▣ Input	Focus Listening	I>WC
● ●	A2 Writing	Transfer	I, PW
●	A3 Vocabulary	Vocabulary Chart	I, PW
●	A4 Practice	Game	GW
●	B1 Vocabulary Input	Discussion	GW>WC
● ●	B2 Vocabulary	Vocabulary Sorting	GW
(● ●)	Optional extra 'Rings and Things'	Information Gap	PW
● ●	C1 Reading	Highlighting	PW
●	C2 Practice	Information Gap	PW
(●●●●●●●)	Optional exercise 'Creative Fruit'	Vocabulary>Creative Writing	PW
● ●	D1 Thematic Input	Gap Fill	I
●	D2 ▣ Vocabulary/Reading	Focus Listening	I
● ●	D3 Vocabulary	Vocabulary Sets/Discussion	PW
● ●	D4 Writing	Transfer	I
●	E1 Thematic Input	Information Gap	I
● ●	E2 Practice/Reading	Discussion	GW
(● ●)	Optional alternative 'Colour Cards'	Discussion	GW
● ●	F Learning To Learn	Ranking/Discussion	GW

NB This is a very full unit – the key here is CHOICE, according to needs and personalities of the class. Hence timing here is more than the 'normal' 90 minutes.

Communicative Functions
Describing things
Describing people

Topics and Vocabulary
Natural things
Personality

Language Focus
Work order
Relative clauses

This unit concentrates on vocabulary extension with emphasis on language of colour, texture, taste and smell.

Materials to photocopy: optional game 'Rings and Things' after B
optional exercise 'Creative Fruit' after C
optional colour cards for Classbook Section E2

Materials to collect: Enough different fruit or vegetables for there to be one between two students. A few sharp knives and some paper towels. For optional exercise 'Creative Fruit'.

Alternative Entry Point: Any Section

A

WHAT'S IT CALLED?

1 ⏺ Individual.

Answers:
1 conversation 1 – father and daughter at home; conversation 2 – customer and salesman in a hardware shop.
2 (left to right) bolt, nut, screw, nut, bolt.

A possible extension here is to discuss the different pronunciation of words such as 'to object/ an object', 'to prospect/a prospect', 'to conduct/ his conduct', etc.

3 Answers:	Object 1	Object 2
Shape	long, thin, flat	circular/hemispherical
Colour	silver	orange
Made of	metal	steel
Size	20mm	35cm 15cm

For vocabulary extension, brainstorm to include in the 'Other words' column such things as triangular, oval, rectangular, etc., colours (see B1), wood, wool, plastic, etc., bigger than, minute, medium-size, etc. For further vocabulary work on shapes, see Resource Book B1, B2 and B3.

4 Object 1 has round bits at each end, like a fork with two prongs, and is for undoing nuts.
Object 2 has a non-stick surface, two parts and two handles, and is for cooking rice.

5 Object 1 is a spanner; **Object 2** is a wok

Conversation 1

Daughter Where is it, Dad?
Father I think it's in the tool box, under the stairs.
Daughter Yes, I've found the tool box, but there are lots of things in it. Which one do you want?
Father Now, be careful. Look in the box. Can you see a strong, blue, plastic case?
Daughter No. Oh yes, here it is.
Father Well, open it and you'll see a lot of long, thin, flat tools of different sizes. I don't want the black ones; I want the silver ones.
Daughter Yes, they're long and thin in the middle and there are sort of round bits at each end, like a fork with two prongs. Heavy!
Father Yes, well they're made of metal! Erm, bring me the largest one.
Daughter It's very big. Do you mean the one with 30mm written on it?
Father Oh, no, I mean the one with 20mm written on it. I'd forgotten I'd bought the big one.
Daughter Here you are, dad. What's it for? How do you use it?
Father It's for undoing nuts.
Daughter Nuts? The ones you eat?
Father [*laughter*] Don't be silly, they're metal nuts, things which you put on bolts.
Daughter Bolts? For locking the door?
Father No, no. Look, you put the tool around the nut and turn. Oh, never mind, I'll show you later.

Conversation 2

Assistant Can I help you, madam?
Woman Oh erm, I'm looking for a cooking pot, a, a special one, but I'm not quite sure what it's called.
Assistant Oh, yes. Erm, well, perhaps you could describe it for me.
Woman Yes, it's made of steel, I think, with a non-stick inner surface.
Assistant Ah. So it's metal and not enamel. [Mm] Erm we have a lot of non-stick pans.
Woman Oh. This one is really in two parts. There are ... there's a, a circular base which supports it on the cooker, and the pan itself is ... is round, sort of.
Assistant Round? [Mm] But all pans are round.
Woman Oh no, I mean the bottom is round. It's sort of hemispherical.
Assistant Oh, like a bowl? [Yes]
Woman Yes, and I think there are two handles.
Assistant Oh! I think I know what you mean! [Oh good] It's for cooking rice ... well, erm, oriental food.
Woman Yes, yes, that's right.
Assistant Here we are, madam. We have the older-style iron ones [Mm] and a modern non-stick pan. Erm, that comes in erm orange only, I'm afraid.
Woman Mm. (Well) They're quite big, aren't they?
Assistant Yes, yes, they're all this size, about erm, 35 centimetres in diameter and erm, (well) 15 centimetres deep. It's here on the box.
Woman It's for a wedding present, you see. Well, I hope that's what my daughter wanted. I'll take the orange, non-stick one. W, what is it called?
Assistant Well, the box says it's ... hang on, a .... it seems to be ...

2 Individual. For further work on word order see Resource Book B1 and B2.

3 Group work. See A1 **3** for possibilities.

4 Group work. Elicit other possible questions before beginning the game. For more exercise on descriptive words see Resource Book B3.

B

COLOURS

1 Group work or whole class. Peoples' perception of colours often varies. This can be an interesting discussion point.

2 Group work. *Plants* – primrose, lavender, magnolia, ginger; *Woods* – ebony, tan, charcoal; *Fruit* – lime, plum, olive, apricot, peach, lemon, burgundy, chestnut; *Precious stones* – ruby, emerald; *Metals* – silver, gold, rust, copper. (Other groupings are possible and may well lead to discussions of personal concepts of items of vocabulary, thus aiding vocabulary retention.)

Optional exercise

'Rings and Things' on page 80. Game. Pair work. The students take it in turns to describe each of the rings on their card to each other. Student A is aiming to find the matching pairs. Student B is aiming to find the rings that are different.

C

MALAYSIAN FRUIT

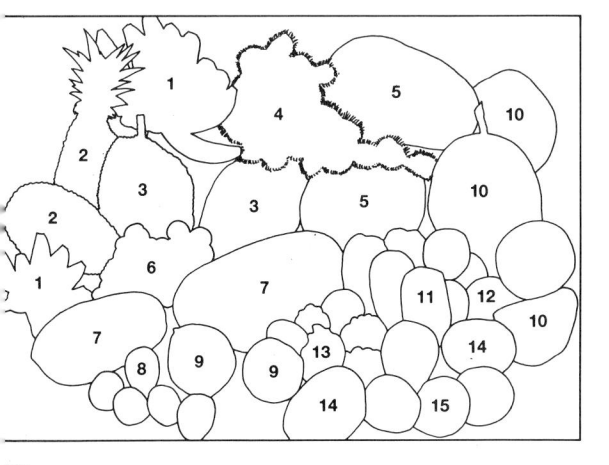

KEY

1 bananas	6 langsat	11 star fruit
2 pineapple	7 papaya	12 lime
3 durian	8 ciku	13 mangosteen
4 rambutan	9 guava	14 mango
5 melons	10 coconut (outside and inside)	15 custard apples

1 Pair work. The note on vocabulary categorization in B2 above also applies for this exercise, e.g. 'creamy' could refer to both taste and texture.

Columns could include:

Smell	Taste	Texture
sweet	fresh	juicy
fresh	delicious	jelly-like
strong	sour	soft
distinctive	distinctive	tender
disgusting	bitter	spiky
mouldy	sweet	creamy
	creamy	crunchy
	tangy	crisp
	mouldy	smooth
	tart/sharp	firm
	watery	squashy

2 Pair work. For possible extension see below.

Optional exercise

'Creative Fruit'. Pair work. Display the fruit and vegetables. Each pair chooses one. Give out the worksheet on page 81, and as students work through, encourage them to take enough time to stretch their vocabulary and imagination. (If necessary 'orchestrate' the changing from one step to another.) *Allowing enough time is crucial.* The writing can be done either in pairs or individually. Time: 1 hour minimum.

D

DESCRIBE YOURSELF

1 Individual. This is aimed at encouraging students to look for new words to describe different objects. You could go through the walk with them, introduce each stage, let them imagine it then write it up for homework. This walk can actually be 'interpreted' and students' descriptions can form the basis of group/class discussion.

the forest	=	your general outlook on life at present, e.g. gloomy? gnarled trees?
the path	=	your direction in life, e.g. clear? straight?
the key	=	yourself, your 'inner' person, e.g. valuable? miserably small?
the bear	=	how you deal with problems, e.g. run away?
the water	=	your attitude to emotions/sex, e.g. deep? murky?
crossing the water	=	how you handle emotions, e.g. jump in? slowly?

the other side = how you view the future, e.g. the same? better?

the building = your need for security. Is it a house? Is it safe?

Do the students find the key? Where?

2 Individual. Suggest that students underline useful descriptive vocabulary as they listen.

3 Pair work to group work

4 Individual. 'Portraits' could be numbered and pinned up around the room. Students then have to guess who they are. For further work on personality adjectives and related nouns and verbs see Resource Book B4 and B5.

E

WHO ARE YOU?

1 Individual. Emphasize that students should not spend a long time thinking about their answers. Get them to jot them down to use in E2.

2 Group work. Students should read the Yellow and Blue descriptions (and the other colours on page 82 if possible). By referring to the answers in E1 students can decide which colours other members of the group belong to. Allow time for this discussion which may well prove stimulating. An alternative strategy is to use the two (seven) descriptions as a jigsaw-reading exercise.

F

LEARNING TO LEARN

Different people have different strategies for learning and this will affect what will happen in the classroom. As a result of this discussion, students will hopefully be both more tolerant of activities which do not seem to fit their personal needs/ways of learning and may have discovered some new ways to try out.

UNIT 5

Approx. Timing	Section	Exercise Type	Classroom Organization
●	A1 Thematic Input/Reading	Information Search	GW
●	A2 Input	Note Making	GW
● ●	A3 Practice	Transfer	GW > WC
●	A4 Practice	Discussion	GW
●	B1 Vocabulary	Matching/Discussion	I, PW > GW
● ●	B2 ▣ Input	Flow Chart Information Search/ Gap Fill	I, PW PW, GW, WC
● ●	B3 Practice/Writing	Transfer	I, PW
● ●	C1 Input	Jigsaw > Matching	PW
● ●	C2 Practice/Writing	Transfer	PW
● ●	D Practice	Transfer/Discussion	PW, GW
● ●	E Learning To Learn	Discussion	GW

Communicative Functions
Comparison
Describing processes

Topics and Vocabulary
Statistics
Developing world
Chewing gum

Language Focus
Passives
Sequencing

The aim of this unit is to use the communicative functions above while discussing the theme of the developing world through the exploitation of statistics.

Materials to photocopy: none

Materials to collect: one or more maps of the world
current newspaper reports on the Developing World

Alternative Entry Points: B, D, E

A

DEVELOPING COUNTRIES

1 Group work. Map of the world on page 24 if necessary. The use of current newspaper reports may help to define concepts about the developing world.

2 Group work. Revision of basic comparisons may be necessary before beginning this section. See also Resource Book B5. Explanation of specialist vocabulary in the table may also be advisable, e.g. GNP = total amount that is produced per head of population in goods and services.

3 Re-formed groups. Useful additional words to put on the board may be: *whereas*, *although*, *it also*, *X differs from Y in that . . .*, *On the other hand X has . . .*, etc.

4 One interpretation of the cartoon might be to see the umbrella of aid from the Western World protecting the otherwise exposed Developing World whilst the latter, in turn, helps keep the Western World 'afloat'.

For further work on linking ideas see Resource Book B6.

B

UP A GUM TREE!

1 Individual or pair work to group work.
Possible answers:
1 forest, copse, thicket, jungle, bush (in New Zealand), etc.
2 from left to right: penknife, flick-knife, dagger; top to bottom: machete, carving knife, breadknife
3 numerous possibilities here: if necessary feed in 'seaport', 'shipment' and 'river boats' which appear in Listening B2

2 Individual or pair work.

Answers: **2** search for trees **3** grooves cut in trunks **4** latex flows into containers **6** strained into kettles **7** heated until thickens **8** poured into wooden moulds **9** cooled with cold water **10a** river boats **10b** trucks.

🔊 Chicle and similar natural gums are gathered by groups of workers who go into the jungle forests. Working from a central camp, they search for trees of the right age. A sapodilla tree, for example, must be over 20 years old to give a good yield of chicle. The latex flows well only in wet, rainy weather. The season for tapping the trees is usually from July through to December. Using a long knife called a machete, the workers cut grooves in the tree trunks. The grooves are made in a zigzag pattern, so that the latex flows slowly down into a container at the base of the tree.

Back at camp, the latex is strained through a cloth into large kettles. Then it is heated slowly until it thickens. Next, it's poured into wooden moulds and cooled with cold, clear water. The blocks are taken out of the jungle in small river boats or by trucks to the nearest seaport for onward shipment. In some areas of Malaysia, the blocks of latex were once taken out of the jungle on the backs of elephants.

3 Pair work, groups. Results of the group work can be put on the board or read out and discussed. Discussion of active/passive voice may well arise here.

C

BY GUM!

1 Pair work. Answers (top to bottom): 3, 7, 9, 6, 2, 4, 1, 5, 10, 8

2 Pair work. This exercise could be done orally rather than written. For further practice of passives of process see Resource Book B1 and B2. For past passives in report form see Resource Book B4 and for past passives in scientific writing see Resource Book B3.

D
INVENTIONS

Pair work or group work. Focus more on content rather than form although a mix between active and passive voice may be useful.

E
LEARNING TO LEARN

1 Achieving realistic targets helps students at this 'difficult' intermediate stage to feel they are making real progress with their learning. A useful NLP (Neurolinguistic Programming) technique is to ask students to visualize the outcome of their learning in terms of a different behavioural pattern, i.e. a student who has difficulties in talking on the telephone in English may picture herself confidently picking up the receiver, standing differently, feeling differently, etc. In other words not only saying what they want to do but saying how it will be when they do it. It is useful to break these mega-goals down into weekly-achievable chunks.

2 Much research has shown that for items to pass into long-term memory, reviewing items as suggested in this section is a good idea. A book full of ideas on useful techniques for memorizing is *Use Your Head* by Tony Buzan.

3 A learning diary including how and what has been learnt as well as how the students feel about both the activities and content (inside/outside the classroom) can help students to see their progress/areas which still need work to achieve their personal goals and perhaps how they could learn more efficiently. It is also useful feedback for the teacher, especially for those less vocal students, if the students agree to the teacher seeing (but obviously not correcting) them.

UNIT 6

Approx. Timing	Section	Exercise Type	Classroom Organization
●	A1 Vocabulary	Vocabulary Sorting	I > PW, WC
● ●	A2 Input	Note Taking	I > WC
●	A3 Practice	Discussion	PW, GW
●	B1 Input/Practice	Discussion	PW, GW
● ●	B2 Practice	Transfer/Discussion	I > GW
(● ● ● ●)	Optional exercise 'Alibi'	Role Play	HH > PW
●	C1 Thematic Input/Reading	Reading/Discussion	GW > I
●	C2 Reading	Highlighting	GW
●	C3 Reading/Vocabulary	Matching	I, PW
● ●	C4 Reading	Thematic Transfer	GW, WC
● ●	D1 Listening	Focus Listening/Note Taking	I
● ●	D2 Practice	Note Taking/Writing	GW
● ●	E Learning To Learn	Discussion	GW

Communicative Functions
Describing past actions and events

Topics and Vocabulary
Customs and beliefs
Myths

Language Focus
Past tenses
Sequencing

The main aim of this unit is to practise past tenses through various kinds of storytelling.

Materials to photocopy: optional exercise 'Alibi' after B2

Materials to collect: old family photos (optional)
Things Fall Apart by Chinua Achebe (optional)

Alternative Entry Points: B, C, E.

A

THE GOOD OLD DAYS?

1 Individual to pair work or group work. See the notes on Unit 4 B2.

2 Answers: washing machines/boiling in a copper; vacuum cleaners/beating carpets by hand; radiators/firewood; delivery vans/horse and cart.

Mrs Hamilton I remember when I was a little girl, erm, oh, we used to have only our Christmas presents, and mother . . . well, she hid 'em under the bed. [Oh . . .] [*laughter*] I can remember very well how I used to go under the bed [*laughter*] an . . . and steal the sweets [*laughter*] that was in beside 'em [*laughter*] . . . That was my early days . . . Yes, and life for women is a lot easier now than it used to be, I think.

Mrs Prior Well, yes, of course. We used to scrub everything, you know, with, you know, a scrubbing brush, down on our knee, an . . . and [Yes . . . oh yes] all that, and (well) you don't have any of that now. Of course you had (No) no machines. You used to have to beat the carpets by hand and . . . Mondays was boiling the whites in the copper.

Mrs Hamilton That's right!

Mrs Prior Kitchen was always full of steam.

Mrs Hamilton Yes. Oh we used to have the brasses to clean. [Yes, that's right] (Yeah) And the grate to clean out! [And the grate . . .] And d'you know, we used to whiten the front door step every day!

Mrs Prior Oh Yes! Oh, real hard work! [Mm] I used to work in a draper's shop and . . . I was only thinking now, recently, it w . . . it was so cold there, you know. Boards on the floor [Oh, yes] no carpet and I got chilblains! Oh, terrible! On my hands. [Mm] I've never had them [Oh!] since. It was so cold there, you know. And we used to take our Thermos of cocoa in the morning and pour this cocoa out and put our hands round the thing to try and get a bit o' warmth, you know. Oh it was terrible 'cause we used to serve calico stuff – people wouldn't [Oh, yes?] know what that was nowadays; but oh it was so (it) cold stuff, you [No] see, and it all gave me chilblains.

Mrs Hamilton Oh yes. I can remember the cold, yes. Oh, and waiting for [Oh, yes] the, for the oil man to call every Tuesday he came, yes. (yeah) . . . He [the oil man . . . yes . . . Tuesday] had a closed-in cart. It was it . . . full of soap and oil and bundles of firewood. He had candles and paraffin . . . Oh, . . . the smell! [firewood] [paraffin, that's right] The van was . . . was pulled by a lovely old horse [Mm] who used to know what house to stop at. [*laughter*] When he reached our house, he used to trot up the path where my mother, or one of the family, was ready with lumps of sugar. Oh, he was a really lovely old horse! [Sugar, yes.]

As an extension students could refer to their list of gadgets from A1 and discuss how many of them were around when they or their parents were young. This is an opportunity to check students' understanding of the difference between the Simple Past and 'used to do'.

For further practice on the Simple Past see Resource Book B3.

3 Pair work or group work followed by class exchange of ideas.

B

STILLS

1 Pair work. If the students haven't seen the films they can imagine what had happened before, what was happening at that particular point in the film and what happened after. Pairs and groups can exchange ideas.

2 Individual > group. This exercise is more effective if the teacher sets the scene well, by taking the students through a 'guided imagery' in the following way: ask the students to close their eyes and imagine themselves finding an old photograph album, in an attic, maybe, or the bottom drawer. Tell them to flip through the pages until they find a picture of two or three people, that they like. Ask them to 'look' at it carefully and remember all they can about it. Ask them to open their eyes and, in groups, take it in turns to explain their photo to other members of the group. Alternatively students can position the other members of the group as in 'their' photograph. The rest of the group try to guess from the positions they are now in, both the relationship of the people in the photo and what was happening, etc.

For further practice in the Past Continuous tense see Resource Book B2.

Optional exercise
For further practice in past tenses see 'Alibi' on page 82. Half half/pair work.

C

TRADITION AND CHANGE

This section makes use of several reading techniques. It is important to ensure that students don't panic at the outset about not understanding every word.

1 Pre-reading discussion. Group work leading to individual skimming and scanning. Emphasize that they are only looking for the information asked for, viz. that everyone has a personal god (chi) over whom the individual, traditionally, has power.

2 Answers: **1** farmer **2** it no longer had pleasure for him **3** that you could influence your 'chi' **4** no **5** personal god/fate/destiny.

3 Individual or pair work. Answers:
1 vigour **2** enthusiasm
3 passion **4** clan **5** personal **6** destiny
7 affirmed **8** yea **9** nay

This text is not only fairly complex linguistically, but also conceptually, and general discussion on spiritual concepts may be helpful at this stage, especially with younger students.

4 Whole class or group work. Possible opportunity for extension into project work. There are many excellent short stories as well as novels in African literature.

D

THE FORBIDDEN FRUIT

With some groups it is helpful to write the African names Ba-atsi and Tahu Tree and ask your students to identify them on the picture.

[🔊] In the beginning God created the first human being, Ba-atsi, with the help of the moon. He kneaded the body into shape, covered it with a skin, and poured in blood. Then, when the man had been given life, God whispered in his ear that he, Ba-atsi, should have children, and he should give them the following warning, 'Of all the trees of the forest you may eat, but of the Tahu tree you may not eat'.

So, Ba-atsi had many children and told them the warning, and then went to heaven.

At first men respected the commandment they had been given and lived happily, but one day a pregnant woman had an irresistable craving for the forbidden fruit. She therefore tried to persuade her husband to get some for her. To begin with he refused, but after a time he gave way. He crept into the wood, picked a tahu fruit, peeled it and hid the peel among the leaves.

However the moon had seen his action and reported it to God. This made God so angry that as a punishment, he sent death to the people.

1 Individual listening and note taking, possibly comparing notes and writing the story in pairs or small groups.

2 Group work. Alternatively students can work in pairs telling each other stories, and then swap partners to retell both stories.

E

LEARNING TO LEARN

We all read many things in many different ways every day of our life. Students can use those same skills when reading in a foreign language. They don't always need to understand every word.

REVIEW

UNIT 2

	Approx. Timing	Section	Exercise Type	Classroom Organization
Part 1 Language Review	●	A1 Thematic Input	Vocabulary Sets	I>PW, GW
	●	A2 Listening/Practice	Focus Listening	I, PW
	●	A3 Listening/Practice	Filling in form	I, PW
	●	A4 Listening	Note Taking	I>GW
	● ●	B1 Thematic Input	Discussion	PW
	●	B2 Listening	Matching	I, PW
	● ●	B3 Listening	Note Taking/Discussion	I>WC
	● ●	C1 Vocabulary/Thematic Input	Creative Writing	PW, GW
	● ●	C2 Listening	Jigsaw	I, PW
	● ●	C3 Listening	Jigsaw	I, PW
	●	D Listening	Highlighting	I>WC
	● ●	E Learning To Learn	Grading	I>GW
Part 2 Simulation	● ●	**Stage 1** Preparation	Discussion	PW>WC
		Stage 2 The problem		
	● ●	1 and 2 Thematic Input	Roleplay	HH, PW
	● ●	3 Listening	Matching/Discussion	PW, WC
		Stage 3 The great debate		
	● ●	1 Preparation	Note Taking	I
	● ●	2 Reading	Highlighting	I, PW
	● ● ● ● ● ● ● ●	3 Debate	Roleplay	WC

Topics and Vocabulary
Britain: people, places and accents

Simulation
Dalelakemoor

The purpose of this unit is to revise and extend the previous three units. Again the Language Review section and/or the Resource Book could be used for diagnostic purposes or for extending functional practice (Classbook) or additional grammatical work (Resource Book).

Materials to photocopy: none
Materials to collect: collection of pictures/postcards of two distinctly different towns in your region/country (optional)
Alternative Entry Points: any section of the Language Review

Simulation

PART ONE

LANGUAGE REVIEW

A

GRANDAD!

1 (*authentic*) Individual > pairs or groups

Steve Me grandad. Me grandad's name, his name's John Curtin, and he comes from like an Irish family; I was telling you before, a lot of the Liverpool people have Irish blood in them. Well, his father died when he was six, and they lived right on the, more or less where everyone lived in them days, right on the docks, you know, the docking area. Well, erm, he left school when he was fourteen to sup . . . you know, to support the family and that, well they had to in them days. And he went working on the barges on the canals. And he went all over England on barges, like you know, Liverpool to Leeds, on that canal or The Manchester Ship Canal and everything. And then he went away to sea and he's been round the world seven times. [Mm]

And he's a real . . . he's a real funny character because, you hear about Liverpool wit and humour, and he is really re . . . Even now he's seventy-five, and he . . . he'll still give you a good laugh and you sit in the pub with him. And at the moment he's working on the door of a pub, and erm, not a pub, a Catholic club in Liverpool.

Me gran . . . Everyone calls him Skip. I don't know why, but even when we were kids, all his mates called him Skip, and he was a docker then. And I can always remember, like, in the . . . the back kitchen, he lived in a two-up two-down in a . . . a district called Kirkdale which is also north Liverpool. (And) he'd come home and get all the kids in the street rounded up and let them all run round the block for tuppence. [*laughter*] This is going back a few years ago, you know, when like tuppence you could buy a few sweets or something for it then.

Erm . . . They were really rough but, like you could leave your front door open. And I can even remember their house, they never locked the front door: and he never answered the front door, he just shouted like, 'Come in', or someone, and the bread . . . the bread man, the milkman, paper lads, anyone'd just walk in the house, you know. And everyone knew each other. And everyone in me Nan's street all knew each other, you know, like this whole community. And I'd love things like to be back like that, but it's never going to be like that.

Erm last year, when it was his birthday, he was on the door of the club, and all the girls in the club erm, chipped in and got him one of these Kissogram girls.

And she was seven . . . seventeen stone! [*laughter*] A seventeen-stone French maid with suspenders on an . . . and all that lark! He was made up. Got photo . . . photograph of him, you know, when she's giving him a kiss and everything. Erm . . .

Angi He enjoyed that?

Steve Oh ay, yeah. I'll tell you what. I remember when he used to take us on his bike, his pushbike, from their house down to the docks. And he was always tormenting us he . . . I remember once he got me down by the warehouses when I was a kid. And he'd run away and s . . . and be saying, 'The bogieman, the genie's coming!' I'd be screaming and crying. And he'd think it was hilarious. But when I'd tell me mam, she'd go absolutely berserk! But he always spoiled us. He was always sort of erm giving us, he'd give us money and . . . When I got a bit older, like sixteen, take us for a pint and that, you know . . .

2 Individual. Answers:

used to do
3 All his mates called him Skip.
5 He let the kids run round the block for tuppence.
6 They never locked the front door.
8 He gave us money.

did
1 He left school at 14.
2 He went all over England on barges.
4 We lived in a two-up two-down.
7 The girls got him one of those kissograms.

NB The statements in these columns relate to the context of the taped extract. Some facts, e.g. 'he went all over England on barges' could be either structure depending on the context.

Note for users of the 2nd edition of the Classbook. The sentences are already in the correct order! Therefore as an alternative you might like to take this opportunity to discuss the tenses which can express past habit *used to*, *would do*, *did*, or tell a 'story from the past' of your own using all three tenses, and ask the students to pick out the three different ways you use to express past habit. If you record yourself telling the story you can afford to let students just enjoy the anecdote on the first listening and replay the recorded version for 'tense' work.

3 Individual or pair work. Answers:
Name: John Curtin
Religion: Catholic
Age now: 75
Home town: Liverpool
Age left school: 14
Jobs: 1 worked on barges
  2 docker
  3 on the door of a Catholic club

4 Individual > group work

B

A TALE OF TWO TOWNS

1 (*authentic*) Pairs. Answers: Liverpool – the docks; Welsh town – mining.

Steve Erm, well it's an industrial city. [Mm] At the moment it's it's a bit down now 'cause a lot of unemployment there. People say it's a pretty run-down area but, I wouldn't say so, it's still got a lot of character there – lot of fine old buildings, art galleries, parks, museums, erm . . . two good football clubs. [*laughter*] Let's see, erm . . . I can't think what else to say . . . erm . . . The town erm the town centre, everything is built around the docks . . .

Angi Tell me about the people . . . the northerners.

Steve Erm, well, not northerners really, because you can't generalize and say Liverpool people are like northerners. Liverpool i . . . is supposed to be the capital of Ireland because, erm ninety per cent of Liverpool people have probably got Irish blood in them somewhere along the line, and erm . . . It's a totally different accent and totally different sense of humour to people. You can go sort of seven, eight miles outside Liverpool and the accent and the sense of humour and everything gets totally different, compared to what Liverpool is. But Liverpool was brought up . . . It was a . . . a big dock and seaport area but everything spread out, the whole city spread out. Instead of everyone living on top of each other around the dock area, it all spread out to sort of new towns and Liverpool people live . . live here.

If I'm correct I think more people have left Liverpool than any other city in Britain, or any other city in Europe for that matter, over the last thirty, thirty-five years. I think Glasgow's had more or less the same problem, becuase you know, boundaries have moved out, haven't they? (And) . . . the the people in like the heart of the city, that population has just dwindled. And like as the industries, well the main industry for Liverpool was the docks, that's left. Erm . . . and once that started going really. I think that was the beginning of the end for the place.

Angi What about the differences then, between Liverpool and here?

Steve It's just erm, it's just erm funny really, because the whole of the north of England, even in the thirties when the depression was on, they suffered a lot more than the south ever did, and it's exactly the same now. And th . . the rift has just become, it can't become any greater really than it is now. And I . . I can understand why the rift's there between the south and the north, especially like London area. Because once you do get north of Watford Gap, it is totally different, and the southerners, the . . . their view of the north is totally . . . They seem to think, the majority of people living in London, seem to think that everyone in the north is sort of living in terraced houses and walking round with clogs on and eating black puddings for breakfast and everything, you know. [Mm] When it's not like that at all. But tha . . that's just their general opinion type thing. Erm, can't see it changing much, mind you. We wouldn't want it to change because erm, the north is a lot mo . . is a lot more of a friendly place than the south, (you know) the people are warmer.

Now here's Leon talking about a Welsh mining town.

Leon Well there's this valley (. . s), in the tow . . in in Wales of course, where else? But it is a town, ay, is a very nice town, or it was in its time, I think. It has a ribbon development with the houses stretching from one end of the valleys to the other: but my God, it's depressing. I mean, if you look at it now, you cannot imagine that it was ever lovely. In fact you have to look up high to really think what it might have been like, and then of course, you get the hills. There they are, the brooding hills, looking down on you all the time. Lots of it green, I mean, it's not all there with slag heaps with grass growing on it. But if you know what you're looking for you can see them as well. But the green at the top spells freedom. I mean, you can go up there, get the wind in your face, and the rain – that's most of the year of course – and you can walk around and you can look down on what was once probably a pleasant place to live. That's when the pits were open, of course. No more, no, good gosh, no more. That's all past. And there's the signs now of nobody every caring about it – sad really. They're trying to get it together. Some money is being spent on things like precincts – oh, we'd never have thought of those years ago – paved areas, well we wouldn't have thought of those either. But they're trying to do that to get a bit of pride back into the valley. Gosh, it needs it. They need money spent on 'em. They deserve it, of course. Generations have left . . . got out, got out indeed into all sorts of jobs. But, those that are left are there to pick up the pieces. With the grey slate rooves – nothing mod about them – and the long winding roads. Lots of houses boarded up these days, and then the derelict pits, top and bottom end of the valley. Once it was a place of pride, now a place of desolation.

2 Individual, pair work. Answers:
art gallery – 4 – Liverpool
boarded-up houses – 1 – Welsh town
docks – 2 – Liverpool
football ground – 6 – Liverpool
grey slate roofs – 9 – Welsh town
pits – 5 – Welsh town
ribbon development – 3 – Welsh town
town centre – 8 – Liverpool (could be Welsh town if students identify the word 'precincts' in Leon's description)
valley and hills – 7 – Welsh town

3 Individual, whole class. Similarities – a lot of unemployment; both are depressing places now; people are leaving both to look for work; people were once proud to live there. Differences – Liverpool was built around docks and has spread out, the Welsh town is an example of ribbon development; Liverpool has more facilities than the Welsh town.

These are obvious examples but depending on interest/class level, a discussion could focus on such things as the Irish population in Liverpool, attempts to regenerate the old industrial areas, etc.

C

TWO TALES

1 Pairs, small groups

2 (authentic) Individual, pair work

First, Dave's story

I remember, erm, the, the sort of the main drag in Glasgow is what they call the High Street, it's the old town, and I was actually a trolley-bus conductor. [Mm] Now when trolley-buses do a sort of sharp left, right-hand turn they're supposed to go quite slowly at ten miles an hour, [Mm] otherwise their so-called booms come off. That's these big poles that go up to the wire. So I was a, a new bus conductor, and this trolley-bus was erm going up the High Street, up to the Glasgow Cathedral sort of area, and it was turning left, for a sort of short terminus, you see. But the guy was in a hurry so he went round the corner too fast, and the booms came off, right? (Well) When that happens the conductor's supposed to fish . . . you know, get a big pole out and fish around for it. But 'cause I was inexperienced in these matters, I was kind of, watching about trying to get this thing back on the wire, erm . . . and he got fed up, the driver that is, he got fed up waiting. So he leapt out of the cab and came back to sort of, erm, do it for me, as it were. And of course we're both raised up there, and then suddenly, to our intense consternation, we realized that the bus was actually rolling backwards? [*laughter*] You see. Now this is only the beginning of this disaster erm . . . So he let go, and of course there, there's quite a tension (erm) going into the overhead wires, you know. [Mm] All these wires lying about the road [Oh dear], erm which o' course they're live, and all the rest of it. [Mm] Meanwhile, a, a van comes round, you know, it was on a kind of crest of a hill on a corner, you know, and it ran into the back of the pole, you see. So my next task then was to persuade the driver of the van that of couse erm, the trolley-bus couldn't possibly be running backwards, [*laughter*] he just crashed into the back of it. Because, you know, when you hit a . . anything from behind, it's always your fault, ain't it? (So I was) busy persuading this guy to do that. Erm, meanwhile the passengers were kind of getting off in a (kind of) disgruntled state because the trolley-bus was going nowhere at this juncture. [*laughter*] Meanwhile two other vehicles tried to get past simultaneously, you know, I was kind of watching across the road, (and) saw that a . . another truck which was full of tomatoes and something else tried to pass and of course, they got wedged, and the back came of and there was tomatoes all over the road. [*laughter*] And erm, at one point shortly after this, I can remember standing there, hanging on to the overhead wire, with, with some skill, 'cause it's not really . . . It's a typical Glasgow thing . . . This guy, he's standing at the side, said, 'This is no job for a man', you know, he'd, go and get his wife to do this for us! [*laughter*] Oh yeah, they were very chauvinist. [*laughter*] And erm, so meanwhile, of course, the traffic jammed up on both sides, and, and what they call the 'Gestapo' in Glasgow, that's the kind of inspectorate, they couldn't get near it at all. So there was a complete traffic jam for miles either way, you know. And so finally when we got back, I'll always remember the driver said, 'Never mind, David (erm) 'twas nabody's fault, nabody's fault'.

And now, Rod's story

Well, I was a crane op. And with the crane op's job went the sort of . . . erm, I don't know, what would you call it? . . . The responsibility of being captain of lifeboat number three, you see. Well, I ain't got a bloody clue how to lower this boat to the sea. I didn't even know how to start the engine on it (you) see. Anyway, we had this superintendent called Jock MacIntyre, I think his name was, or Jock MacIntosh, I can't remember. But, erm, he was a right sod to get on with, you know, he was a rig superintendent. And he turned up on the rig one day, and sort of their word is God, Whatever happ . . whatever they say, happens. And he decided to have an 'abandon rig' drill. So, we were all having lunch one day and this, this alarm goes off, 'Abandon rig! Abandon rig!'. So the function of the captain of lifeboat number three, and, he's not on his own, he's got the chief derrickman with him – you're the only two guys on, on this lifeboat. But, first of all you get lifeboat one and lifeboat two, take every single part of the personnel off the rig, that's everybody, and that leaves just myself and the chief derrickman on the rig, OK? And what we're supposed to do is to go round the entire rig and check that no one's left on board. Now can you imagine it, just two guys left on the rig? This thing's supposed to be blowing up, catching fire, Christ knows else, you know, what is going to happen to it, and they expect us two to stay on, on the rig and look round! Sod you, no one's going to do that: we went straight to the lifeboat. So, when we get there, this guy says, 'Right, let's get going.' I says, 'Well, how d'you start it up?' He says. 'D . . Don't you know?' I says, 'I don't even know how to get the bloody thing to the water.' So, we was stood there trying to work out what we're going to do, see? So in the end we were just stood there thinking, 'Well, what's going to happen here?' And all of a sudden this door flung open, all right? And there's this bloody great Texan stood there, I mean, this guy was six foot six, built both ways, stood there and all he had on was a pair of hobnailed boots and a tin hat and he was crying, he was saying, 'They've left me, the bastards have left me!' [*laughter*] And we just stood there and we cracked up laughing, we couldn't help it. But the way we got out of it was we smashed the spark plugs and then, as soon as the other two boats came back, I mean, they give us a right ticking off, you know, 'Where the friggin hell were you?'. I says, 'Well, look, you know, we couldn't get the boat to the water, because the, the spark plugs were smashed, we couldn't even start the engine.' So we got out of it that way. But as soon as they sent a mechanic up to fix it, like he had to put these plugs in, and then check the engine and check all the lowering gear, you know, I watched him how he done it, so I wouldn't forget a second time. So . . . I got away with it . . . I could've got run off. (But) it was fun!

Answers:
trolley-bus story – **3, 4, 5, 7, 10, 12**
lifeboat story – **1, 2, 6, 8, 9, 11**

3 Individual, pairs. Answers:
trolley-bus story – **3, 5, 10, 7, 4, 12**
lifeboat story – **8, 1, 11, 6, 2, 9**

D

WHERE ARE THEY FROM?

Individual, whole class
1 Liverpool **2** Wales **3** Glasgow **4** London

This is a good chance to discuss the varieties of English students may hear, and analyze what is 'correct' English. If there is a strong accent/dialect in your area get the students to bring examples into the classroom for discussion/comparison.

Extract 1
I remember once he got me down by the warehouses when I was a kid. And he'd run away and s . . and be saying, 'The bogieman, the genie's coming!' I'd be screaming and crying. And he'd think it was hilarious. But when I'd tell me mam, she'd go absolutely berserk!

Extract 2
. . . but my God, it's depressing. I mean, if you look at it now, you cannot imagine that it was ever lovely.

Extract 3
So I was a, a new bus conductor, and this trolley-bus was erm going up the High Street, up to the Glasgow Cathedral sort of area, and it was turning left, for a sort of short terminus, you see. But the guy was in a hurry so he went round the corner too fast, and the booms came off, right?

Extract 4
Well, I was a crane op. And with the crane op's job went the sort of . . . erm, I don't know, what would you call it? . . . The responsibility of being captain of lifeboat number three, you see.

E

LEARNING TO LEARN

Encourage the students to look at how they have assessed themselves and, for items not graded 'very well,' ask them to decide if they want to know the item better. If they do, suggest that they work out for themselves the best way of doing that. The Resource Book, if it has not already been used, may be useful here.

PART TWO

SIMULATION

DALELAKEMOOR

Whole class. As an introduction compare National Parks in the UK and students' own countries. In Britain there are 10 National Parks which are areas protected and maintained by a government body. They have very strict rules dating from the 1949 National Parks Act which had two primary objectives:
1 '... the preservation and the enhancement of the natural beauty of the Park'
2 '... the promotion of the Park's enjoyment by the public'
NB Make sure that students are clear that in the UK people live and work in National Parks. In many countries this is not so.

Stage 1 Pair work > whole class. Look at the map carefully and explain any vocabulary, e.g. 'quarries', 'reservoirs', etc. Problems for Dalelakemoor include encroachment of tourism, military encroachment, etc. Using the blackboard or overhead projector to brainstorm ideas on possible critical problems will be useful preparation for the simulation later. Areas covered might include: noise (cars, speedboats, etc.); litter; ice-cream/hamburger vans; ugly, conspicuous campsites/chalets, etc; severe traffic congestion; hordes of tourists; pressure on car parking space; damage to farming (especially in the lambing season); great problems with the free-roaming native ponies; footpath erosion, etc., etc.

Stage 2 Half half > pair work. The organizations may need explaining. Graphics on the side of the page will help. Note that the oak tree is the symbol of the National Trust. Any leaflets brought in would be useful for preparation work here.

Interviewer Good evening and welcome to *Comment*. Now I'm sure, as you know, the local council is proposing wide-sweeping changes to our local National Park, and this has caused a good deal of debate. So, in the studio this evening, I have as my guests, Stevie Turner from the local council, and Joan Vickers who represents several local conservation groups, to put forward their points of view. So, first of all, Stevie, could I ask you what your feeling is about these propositions?
Stevie Ah well, my feeling is erm, very very positive. Erm, I think that erm the proposals will enhance the general beauty of the park ... [Mm] enormously. Erm, also erm we'll be able to bring in a lot of workers to erm, to deal with the new changes that are being made. And so a lot more work will be brought into the area. Erm, everyone should be allowed to enjoy parks, erm, and I think that after these new changes, they will.
Interviewer Good, Joan, you ... I can see you don't agree with that.
Joan Not at all. I ... in fact I've got completely the opposite opinion, I'm afraid. We've seen this kind of redevelopment happening in parks all over the world. You get commercialization ... They are redeveloped. And instead of being beautiful leisure centres where one can go and have a lovely day out, they become noisy, ugly, they proliferate with campsites and litter ... (Well, yes ah ...
Stevie ... Can I come in here, please? ... Erm, ah Joan, I'm not sure if you've actually seen the plans, the layout that we're proposing to erm, to put forward for the changing of the of the park. Erm, you know, so I'm not sure whether you can actually comment on this. Of course erm these sort of terrible things can happen to beautiful places, places. But, erm, we will make sure that the campsites will be controlled, erm, they will be inconspicuous. Erm, there's plenty of litter bins around, people I think are generally responsible and respect ... the natural beauty ...
Interviewer So what you're saying, Stevie ... is that there'll be planning to ensure that the ... there is no despoil ... despoilation of the area?
Stevie ... Absolutely, of course.
Joan ... Well, you see th .. that's, that is fine in theory. That is wonderful in theory. But in practice people are not generally as responsible as you make out. It would be lovely if it were true but in Dalelakemoor I would be extremely surprised. People will gravitate towards souvenir shops, which we will have everywhere, and all that'll happen is it'll turn into a big, Blackpool type of place ...
Stevie Well, yes, I ... I think that there's a matter for very careful planning here, and erm, of course the council don't intend spoiling the moor, as I said. We want to make it available for more people to enjoy and I think people will respect that privilege.
Joan Well, let's hope so. But to leave that at the moment and to go on to a next point that worries the conservation groups very very strongly is ... Erm, the proposal the ... the Forestry Commission are making which is to plant pine trees as a new development. Now, pine trees, as you know, create even more problems. They spoil the environment. The flora and fauna vanish and birds of course, as you know – and we're we're full of birds at the moment in Dalelakemoor – there's one of the great charms of the place, will be unable to roost in pine trees! Well yes, yes, absolutely ...
Stevie ... Erm, yes, the Forestry Commission have tended to plant pine trees in the past. Yes, (they're) they're very quick growers, they fill out the landscape erm, ah beautifully but, but, yes, I agree, birds, erm, flora and fauna do, do tend to find it difficult, erm,

and we're going to change that now. Th . . th . . there's new, new methods for planting new, different sorts of trees, all sorts of trees are going to be planted. We we'd we will not spoil the environment with only pine trees. And I think that the the animals and the birds that are living in Dalelakemoor will be able to . . to . . to rest very happily erm, in the new natural surroundings [Joan . . .] that they will find there.

Joan Yes, I . . I do, well, I mean I have to take your word for it, but I hope that'll be
⎧true . . . but you see . . .
⎩Well it is . . .

Stevie . . . I'm telling you that it is.

Joan Well, let's go on to another very important point, if I may . . . Erm . . .

Interviewer Yes, indeed . . .

Joan . . . The other aspect that, that is of great concern to us is the historical aspect. As you know, there are pre-historic sites on the moor of the greatest importance. And they are an attraction to many many people, and give people absolute, boundless, limitless [Mm] pleasure. [Mm] How do you intend to protect them?

Interviewer Erm, could I just come in there? As I understand this, this is the proposal to flood the valley. Erm. Princeside Valley I think it's called, isn't it, which has, I believe, several rare historical sites on it . . .

Joan Exactly. And in my opinion that is absolutely disastrous! I mean, they will be destroyed if the valley is flooded. And they are, as you know, absolutely irreplaceable? [Mm]

Stevie Well yes, I . . I of course erm, I understand your concern there – it is a problem. Erm, on the other hand, erm, we all need water. We know th . . that here in Dalelakemoor every year erm we have a drought. Now, we need a reservoir and, may I just say that, erm, reservoirs can be places of great natural beauty . . .

Joan That may be so but may I add that we would have had a much more beautiful place if Dalelakemoor had been left as it was without that reservoir providing the natural beauty but . . . Let me go on to one other thing. Erm, are the . . .

Interviewer Very quickly because we're running out of time.

Joan Right. Well, just to conclude this. Are the Water Board – and this is the big question – are they responsible enough, do they care enough to landscape the site for the benefit both of the flora and fauna lost because of the pine trees and the building of the reservoir? [Stevie?]

Stevie Well, yes [please . . .] yes, if I could just say, yes, I understand that this will be so.

Joan Well, I . . I suppose I have to say that's something. It . . it remains to be [Believe me.] proved . . .

Interviewer Thank you very much, Stevie Turner and Joan Vickers. Thank you.

Points raised in the tapescript include:
National Parks are for everyone.
National Parks provide work for local people.
Campsites are noisy. People leave litter. Cheap souvenir shops proliferate.
Forestry Commission tends to plant quick-growing conifers for financial reasons rather than replacing with traditional but slow-growing, mixed forest.
Pre-historic sites are destroyed by reservoirs, military use, lack of good planning, etc.

Stage 3 Whole class. Pre-roleplay discussion may be useful here.
What sort of tourists do you think the conservationists object to?
What problems may arise in the Park because employment related to tourism is often seasonal?, etc.
1 Individual. Students can either take roles or be themselves, but make sure that the class is fairly evenly divided between those in favour of tourism in the National Parks and those against.
2 Once students have decided on roles give time to study proposed changes, i.e. Water Board official will be in favour of flooding Princeside Valley whereas the Historical Society will not.
3 Teacher could act as chairperson. If enough time is available students could prepare speeches (at home) to present at the debate.
For classes of over 12 either invent other roles (e.g. Director of Leisure Centre International; an official from the Department of the Environment; representative from the 'Friends of Dalelakemoor', etc.) or open up the debate to members of the public and include a reporter from the local newspaper and/or radio station.

Students could also write up a report of the proceedings of the debate from their point of view; make a radio (audio cassette) or TV (video) programme or present an 'exhibition' with posters, articles, use of graphics, etc. to present their case.

UNIT 7

Approx. Timing	Section	Exercise Type	Classroom Organization
●	A1 Thematic Input	Reading/Information Search	I, PW > WC
●	A2 Vocabulary Input	Discussion	PW > WC
●	A3 Thematic Input	Discussion	I, PW, GW
●	Optional exercise 'Voluntary Help Agencies'	Discussion	I, PW, GW
●	B1 Input	Focus Listening-chart	I, PW
● ●	B2 Input	Note Taking/Ranking	I > GW
●	B3 Practice	Information Gap	PW
●	B4 Practice	Roleplay/Game	GW
(● ●)	Optional exercise 'Advice/Problem'	Roleplay/Game	GW
(● ● ● ●)	Optional exercise 'Roleplay'	Roleplay/Writing	GW > I > PW
● ●	C1 Input	Focus Listening/Matching/Note Taking	I, PW > WC
●	C2 Input	Focus Listening/Gap Fill	I, PW > WC
●	C3 Practice	Roleplay	PW
●	C4 Thematic Extension	Discussion	GW
●	D1 Vocabulary Input	Ranking	I > WC
●	D2 Practice	Discussion	GW, WC
●	D3 Reading	Note Taking > Discussion	GW
● ●	E Learning To Learn	Discussion	I, GW

Communicative Functions
Asking for and giving advice

Topics and Vocabulary
Advice agencies
Protecting your home
'Neighbourhood Watch'

Language Focus
Modals: should/ought to
Gerund

This unit focuses on the various agencies that give help to the public in the UK, e.g. The Citizens Advice Bureau, The Samaritans and the police.

Materials to photocopy: optional extra: 'List of voluntary agencies/charities in the UK' for A3
optional exercise: 'Problem/Advice' game for B4
optional exercise: 'Roleplay' for B4

Materials to collect: optional pamphlets on the Citizens Advice Bureau, Samaritans or other 'help' agencies such as Help The Aged, Playgroups, The Salvation Army, etc., that are found locally.

Alternative Entry Points: B, C, E.

A
CITIZENS ADVICE BUREAU

It is often possible to arrange for a volunteer from the Citizens Advice Bureau or other similar agency to come in and talk to a group of students. There are many voluntary agencies in the UK. Some provide general advice whilst others are more specialized, e.g. Alcoholics Anonymous, NSPCC, RSPCA or RNLI. Some receive small grants from the government but all rely on voluntary contributions raised by holding flag days, sponsored walks, fun runs, etc.

1 Individual, pair work > whole class. The Citizens Advice Bureau is a general advice agency.

2 Pair work > whole class. Possible answers:

Housing – Local Council offices, SHELTER; Salvation Army
Social Security – Department of Health & Social Security
Employment – Job Centres; Department of Employment; Industrial Tribunals; Ombudsman, etc. (depending on the nature of the problem)
Redundancy – as above and/or Building Societies or Bank Managers
Consumer Queries – shop where item was purchased; Office of Fair Trading
Disablement benefits and aids – Department of Health & Social Security; British Legion
Pensions – Department of Health & Social Security; Department of Employment; Bank Managers; Insurance agencies
The Law – Police station; Solicitors; Community Legal Aid Centres
The family – Marriage Guidance Council; Family Planning Association; NSPCC: Department of Health & Social Security
Medical Treatment – Health Centres; local doctors' surgery; local hospital
Education – Local Education Office; Headteacher of particular school
HP Agreements – shop where agreement was signed; Solicitors.

NB These organizations are only some of the possibilities. The Citizens Advice Bureau will listen to the nature of the individual problem/query before making any specific recommendation.

3 Discussion. This is intended to highlight a more general look at voluntary agencies. Any materials/pamphlets, etc. brought in could be usefully discussed here.

Optional extra
'List of voluntary help agencies/charities in the UK', page 83.

B
ASKING FOR AND GIVING ADVICE

1 Individual, pair work.

Conversation 1
1st Man Oh, it was like getting blood out of a stone! Have you taken 4B yet today?
2nd Man No, I've got that joy to come! Last period this afternoon what's more. Sometimes I wonder if it's all worth it.
1st Man Yes, I know what you mean, but they're all right really, most of the time.
2nd Man Well, I really think I've had about enough, I want out. I've been looking in *The Times Ed*. But I fancy a complete change really. What do you think I should do?
1st Man Are you serious? That seems rather drastic.
2nd Man Yeah, really I've had enough – lousy pay, no prospects of promotion. I'll be stuck here for the rest of my life with 4B! No, thanks!
1st Man Well then, why don't you follow up one of those adverts for financial consultants, eh? With your mathematical expertise you could do well.
2nd Man Well, yeah, I suppose I could look into it. Yeah, thanks.
1st Man But I think you'd be crazy to. I mean these days if you've got a secure job, hang on to it, that's what I say!

Conversation 2
Presenter Good afternoon and welcome to *From Your Point Of View*. As usual we have our resident legal adviser, Robert Pym, in the studio with us. And our first call today is from Mrs Tyson from Wiltshire . . .
Pym Good morning, Mrs Tyson. How can we help you?
Tyson Well, it's a bit silly really, but I'm getting rather fed up with the children next door. You see, there are always footballs in my garden and little boys ringing at the front door asking for them back. I feel like keeping the balls to teach them a lesson.
Pym Hmm, I understand how you feel, but I wouldn't advise you to do that. Legally you are obliged to give

the ball back no matter how many times they kick it in your garden . . . and it must be in the condition in which you found it.
Tyson Oh, I see. Oh well, I suppose I'll just have to put up with it then.
Pym Might I suggest that you talk to the parents?
Tyson Well, actually I have but I could try again. Thank you anyway.
Presenter (Well) That was an interesting one. Now here's Mr Hawkins from Newcastle with another query.
Pym Hello, Mr Hawkins. How can I help you?
Hawkins Erm, yes, good morning. It's like this. There's this old tree in my garden and it's blocking all the light. So, I want to have it cut down and landscape that bit of the garden, you know? But my next door neighbour says she's going to stop me doing it. Surely she can't do anything, can she? After all it is my garden!
Pym This isn't as straightforward as it seems, I'm afraid. Some trees can have a preservation order put on them by the local council thus preventing their destruction. So, your best course of action would be to find out first of all if your neighbour is right, and if your tree is old enough or special enough to be in this category.
Hawkins Can't I go ahead and get the tree felling people in then?
Pym Well, it would be in your interest to find out your legal position before proceeding with your plans.
Hawkins Well, it doesn't seem right! But I suppose I'd better check up first. Thank you for your help.
Pym You're welcome.
Presenter Well, it's a good idea to safeguard the nation's older tress but it does seem a bit hard on people like Mr Hawkins. Now our next call from Mrs . . .

Conversation 1
Place: Staffroom
Relationship: Colleagues
Problem: Job dissatisfaction
Advice: Change jobs but unwise to give up security.

Conversation 2
Place: Radio programme
Relationship: Expert on phone-in and caller
Problem: Ball in garden/Garden tree
Advice: Give ball back
Check if tree has a preservation order on it

2 Individual

Asking
What do you think I should do?
Surely she can't . . . ?

Giving
Why don't you . . . ?
But I think you'd be crazy to . . .
I wouldn't advise you to do that.
Might I suggest you. . . .
Your best course of action is . . .

Accepting
I suppose I could look into it.
Yes thanks.
Thank you for . . .
I have but I could try again.
I suppose I'll just have to put up with it then.
I suppose I'd better . . .

Refusing
It doesn't seem right.

For other phrases see Language Summary in the Resource Book. For further practice see Resource Book B1 and B2.

3 Pair work. Refer to phrases in B2.

4 Small groups. This exercise often leads to discussion on social problems or British life, e.g.
1 single/young people's housing problems and Social Security rules about residence.
2 different gadgets in the kitchen; rights of the consumer, etc.

Optional exercises
Game 'Problem/Advice' page 84, and/or 'Roleplay' page 85.

'Problem/Advice'. Group work. Organize the students into groups of three or four and give each group a set of problem and advice cards.

Student A turns over a problem card and tells the other group members.
Students B, C and D take an advice card each, and use the language shown to give appropriate advice. Student B then takes the next problem card. Students C, D and A take the advice cards, and repeat.

Time: 10 minutes.

'Roleplay'. Group work. In groups of four (for uneven numbers either leave out the sister or create other siblings), each student takes one of the family roles. Set the scene, e.g. breakfast or dinner table family argument. Ask the students to play their roles so that it could be clear to an observer how each member of the family felt.

Improvise the scene.
Each member of the family then writes a letter to a personal friend complaining about the difficult family situation and asking for advice.
The letters can then be 'posted' across the room to any student who has finished their own letter. She or he then answers as the friend giving advice.

Time: 30–40 minutes. Replies could be done for homework.

C

WATCH OUT! THERE'S A THIEF ABOUT!

1 (authentic) Individual, pairwork > whole class

Erm, if you're going away you must be especially ca . . erm careful of persons who may break into your house. Whilst you're in, it is most unlikely that erm a thief would break in and try to steal from you, al . . although this possibility can't be ignored. However, as soon as you go out, the opportunist may well be trying to get in, even though you're only out for a short while. So, when leaving, make sure that all the windows, er . . erm are closed, especially those that are easily accessible by climbing onto flat roofs or erm climbing up drainpipes; and those that are hidden from view of your friends and neighbours and persons passing by. So check the back of the house as closely as you would check the front of the house. No number of locks and bolts on the front door are any good if you don't shut the back door, or if you hide a key under the mat or under a flowerpot where anybody could find it. If you're going away for a longer period of time, take steps to make sure that the house (looks) occupied and henceforth deters the thief and erm hopefully . . . prevents him from breaking into your house. For instance you must remember to stop the newspapers, and leave a few lights on, and if you have a timer, arrange for the timer to switch lights on and off at various parts of the house, so that it appears to a passer-by that people are in residence. If you've got a good neighbour or, or a nearby relative, then ask them to come to the house every day, check around, make sure everything's OK, open and close windo . . . erm and close curtains, and switch on and off lights. And obviously they will also water your plants and feed your pets and everything else while they're there, if they're as good a friend as you thought they were. Also, be aware that the opportunist thief doesn't carry his tools and swag bag with him as the erm popular image portrays. He'll be looking for the tools in your house. It might be a garden spade or a screwdriver or a hammer, so, if you're going away, lock those away so . . somewhere inside the house so that he can't find them. And if you're away for several weeks, don't bother locking all the internal doors in the hope that you'll deter him from getting around the house having gained entry, because once he's in, the determined thief will cause untold damage breaking down the doors again in order to see what's behind them, because he'll think you've got something to hide.

1 All the pictures relate to points mentioned by the policeman except the one in the bottom right-hand corner, 'letting strangers in'.
2 Leave an extra light on if you go away./Fit a timer switch.
Ask a neighbour to check the house.

It may be useful to extend this discussion by further reference to the pictures, i.e. not letting 'gasmen' in unless they produce identity cards.

2 Individual, pair work. Refer to tapescript.
Answers:
1 . . . persons who may break into your house
2 . . . when leaving, . . . all the windows are closed
3 . . . stop the newspapers
4 . . . the opportunist thief doesn't carry his tools
5 . . . locking all the internal doors

3 Pair work

D

CRIME IN YOUR LOCAL AREA

1 Individual > whole class

2 Discussion. Groups or whole class

3 Small groups > whole class. If students have problems in thinking of ideas the list below contains the advantages of the Neighbourhood Watch Scheme according to the rest of the official pamphlet:

– the result of Neighbourhood Watch schemes already established show that they can help to reduce local crime such as burglary, vandalism, car theft and thefts from cars
– a better community spirit can be created

- suspicious strangers waiting outside schools, in parks and playgrounds where children congregate, can be quickly reported to the police
- crime prevention advice can be quickly and efficiently circulated throughout the community
- Neighbourhood Watch schemes lead to a greater shared awareness of the problems in your community and to a better understanding of the practical steps that can be taken to tackle these

E

LEARNING TO LEARN

We all listen to many different things in many different ways every day of our life. Students can use those same strategies when listening in a foreign language. They don't always need to understand every word.

UNIT 8

Approx. Timing	Section	Exercise Type	Classroom Organization
• •	A1 Input	Focus Listening/Gap Fill	I, PW
•	A2 Practice	Information Gap/Discussion	PW
•	A3 Vocabulary	Matching	I, PW, GW
• •	A4 Practice	Discussion	GW
• •	B1 Input	Focus Listening/Note Taking	I, PW>WC
	B2 Input	Chart/Ranking	I, PW>WC
•	B3 Practice	Discussion	GW
(• • • •)	Optional exercise 'Agreement Cards'	Practice/Discussion	GW
•	C1 Input	Matching	I, PW>WC
• •	C2 Reading	Discussion	GW
•	D1 Input/Practice	Language Chart/Transfer	I, PW>WC
• •	D2 Transfer	Roleplay	PW
• •	D3 Practice	Questionnaire	PW>M
(• • • •)	Optional exercise 'The Trouble With The World Today'	Roleplay	GW
• •	E Learning To Learn	Discussion	GW

Communicative Functions
Asking for and giving opinions
Agreeing and disagreeing
Expressing no opinion

Topics and Vocabulary
Modern life
Issues and causes

Language Focus
Link words
Neither/Either

The point of this unit is to give students the language for discussing the issues they feel strongly about.

Materials to photocopy: optional game: 'Agreement Cards' for B3
optional roleplay: 'The Trouble With The World Today' for D3

Materials to collect: newspaper headlines
Alternative Entry Points: D3, E

A
STREET INTERVIEWS

1 🔊 Individual or pair work

Interviewer What do you think of modern art?
Girl I like it. It's colourful and exciting, an example of our colourful times.
Interviewer Thank you . . . Excuse me, sir, [Eh?] what's your opinion of modern buildings?
Old man Well, actually I, I hate them, Th . . . the . . . they're too high, and all that glass and concrete looks terrible. They're ugly. Really I, I prefer the old days when (. . . things were in proportion . . .)
Interviewer E . . excuse me, madam. I see you have a lot of shopping. What's your opinion of supermarkets?
Woman Oh, erm, well, erm, I haven't really thought about it so I don't really know. Erm, I suppose they're a good idea. They're cheaper and more convenient because everything is in the same place, but they're too large for my liking and I hate all that canned music. Oh everything is pre-packed too. Me, I, I think I prefer the old-fashioned markets.
Interviewer Excuse me. What do you think of pop music?
Man Well, in my opinion it's awful. [*laughter*] But erm perhaps that's because I'm too old for all that noise! Erm, I'm afraid I'm a bit past it. [*laughter*] But, erm, well young people need something of their own and I, I suppose music is a, is a (way of expressing themselves . . .)

Questions:
1 What do you think of modern art?
2 What's your opinion of modern buildings?
3 What's your opinion of supermarkets?
4 What do you think of pop music?

Answers:
1 I like it. It's colourful and exciting, an example of our colourful times.
2 I hate them. They're too high, and all that glass and concrete looks terrible. They're ugly.
3 I haven't really thought about it so I don't really know. I suppose they're a good idea. They're cheaper and more convenient because everything is in the same place, but they're too large for my liking and I hate all that canned music. . . . Me, I think I prefer the old-fashioned markets.
4 Well, in my opinion it's awful but perhaps that's because I'm too old for all that noise! I'm afraid I'm a bit past it! . . .

2 Pair work

3 More than one answer may be relevant in this exercise. It is a good idea to expand on appropriate vocabulary, i.e. the constant use of 'nice' in English, etc. Items of vocabulary are far more meaningful if contextualized, e.g. badly made –
'the suit was badly made'
'the building was well constructed'

4 Small groups. Discussion.

B
A TELEVISION INTERVIEW

1 🔊 Individual, pair work > whole class

Interviewer Good evening. My guest tonight is Mr Nigel Denton, [Hello] the reporter, critic and lay preacher. You've just written a book about the problems facing young people today, and I understand you have some very strong feelings about this.
Denton Yes, yes indeed. Erm, as you have read in my book, I've travelled a great deal in my life and it's become very clear to me that there is an enormous amount of pressure on young people these days, from all sorts of areas in life. Now, more than ever, I think they need some kind of erm guidance and support. Now one of the ways they can find this guidance is is through education. Erm, it's become increasingly obvious to me that education plays a vital part in in this particular process.
Interviewer How do you feel about the education of young people?
Denton Well, erm I know a lot of people will disagree with me when they when I say this but schools simply aren't strict enough these days. Erm, if children have too much freedom then later on in life they find that they have no responsibility for what they do and that is where erm we get all kinds of crimes and (and) unfortunate behaviour cropping up. Erm it seems to me that it's really not only the the parents' responsibility but the teachers' responsibility as well t . . . to discipline children at an early stage in their lives. Erm, after all if . . if they know what their limits are then they're better erm erm better placed to distinguish between between right and wrong.
Interviewer Perhaps you're thinking of some of the more violent young people. What do you think about football violence?
Denton Well, it's erm what can one say? It . . it's crazy! Erm, b . . on the other hand human beings

are crazy and erm erm fighting is is obviously a part of human nature. [Indeed] Erm of course, on the other hand, erm I think the authorities should be tougher on on hooligans. Erm, my own view is really that if if we were more strict with children erm in their education at an early stage we could prevent this kind of behaviour from happening. Erm, so clearly, on this particular issue there are no easy answers.

Interviewer Well now, I'm afraid we're nearly out of time, but I've just one more question to ask you. <u>What are your views on young people living together before they're married?</u>

Denton Erm you're talking about trial marriage, are you? [Yes] Erm, well th . . my immediate reaction, my instinctive reaction is that that of a preacher, which erm is that vows are made for life before God and erm that really should be the main factor in in people's decision as to whether or not they live together. O . . On the other hand it it is quite clear that trial marriage allows young people erm to learn a little more about each other before they take the final step an . . and that can only be a good thing [Mm] if it's to prevent erm disaster from happening later on in their lives. Erm, at the same time as saying that I'd like to emphasize that it shouldn't be taken lightly though, it is a a serious commitment and should be taken as seriously a . . as marriage itself.

Interviewer Well, I'm afraid our time has run out. Our thanks to Nigel Denton and thank you for being with us, and I hope you can join us at the same time next week. Good night.

The three questions as marked in the tapescript above.

2 Whole class. This is a chance for further practice on appropriate use of intonation. Politeness/impoliteness does not depend solely on structures used but also on such things as body language, distance and intonation. In general the fall-rise intonation is more deferential than other tonal patterns.

3 Discussion. Ensure that students are using the structures and intonation patterns highlighted previously.

Optional extra
'Agreement Cards' on page 85. Small groups. Give one set of the cards to each group. Each set is put in the middle face down. The students take it in turns to pick up and read one of the cards. Other group members must agree/disagree with the opinion on the card. The holder of the card should defend the opinion on the card.

C

1 Individual, pair work > whole class.

Questions	Answers
Don't you think there's too much traffic . . .	Yes, I agree, But don't you think it's necessary . . . ?
It seems to me that we spend too much . . .	I don't completely agree with you . . .
Wouldn't you agree that people don't care . . . ?	That's not quite true . . .
Wouldn't you say that everybody . . .	Yes, but what about . . . ?

The answers are diplomatic because they show alternative ways of partial agreement which is a useful strategy for conversations when there is a need to be non-direct, i.e. politicians and the art of understatement, etc. This exercise could be usefully extended by giving alternative questions to which the students have to answer diplomatically.

2 Small groups. Use current newspaper headlines if possible.

NB In the UK most babies are born in hospitals.
'Duke' refers to The Duke of Edinburgh who is the President of the World Wildlife Fund.
Moves to introduce Peace Studies into schools in the UK have met with political opposition.

Much profitable discussion can be generated by newspaper headlines. It is also useful to discuss the language of newspaper headlines, i.e. use of the present tense; phrasal verbs; lack of articles, etc., e.g. 'Terrorist jailed for 25 years' = A terrorist has been/was jailed for 25 years.

D

I DON'T REALLY KNOW . . .

1 Individual, pair work > whole class. See the Language Summary in the Resource Book for further phrases.

2 Pair work. For further practice in the language of asking for and giving opinions see Resource Book B1 and B2.

3 Pair work > Melée. This exercise gives practice in asking questions as well as reviewing the rest of the language in the unit. It could therefore be used for diagnostic purposes.

Optional exercise
'The Trouble With The World Today' Roleplay page 86.

Groups of four. Each person is given a copy of one of the role cards and time to read and check understanding. Tell the students that they are now the person on their role card and that they must remember their question and how they feel about things. This is to avoid students simply reading out loud. So give them a little more time, if necessary, to read their cards. To help them get into character you could ask them to tell each other (as their new character) what their favourite time of day is; what they usually do on Sunday mornings; what they like to eat; what their favourite book is; etc (keep this very quick). Then when they have a picture of each other's new character (and have built up a picture of their own) take in the role cards and get them to ask and discuss the opinion questions in character.

E

LEARNING TO LEARN

1
1 Making grammatical mistakes does not stop the communicative effectiveness of what you are saying.
2 Making a mistake when you write only feels more serious because it is permanently recorded.
3 True. Making mistakes is a necessary part of learning.
4 Learning is not just a question of accuracy but of fluency and both need to be catered for.
5 Yes, there are times for correction but in the middle of a good conversation is not one of them.

2 It is pointless to feel any of these feelings about making a mistake. Ideally one should feel interested and seize the learning opportunity.

3 Any and all these methods are a normal part of a typical learning situation.

UNIT 9

Approx. Timing	Section	Exercise Type	Classroom Organization
•	A1 Thematic Input	Gap Fill/Discussion Reading	I, PW>WC
• •	A2 Vocabulary Input	Discussion	PW>WC
•	A3 Input	Discussion	GW>WC
(• •)	Optional exercises 1 (extension)	Transfer/Discussion	GW>WC
(• •)	2 'Animal Noises'	Transfer/Discussion	PW>WC
•	B1 ▭ Thematic Input	Focus Listening	I, PW>WC
•	B2 Input	Language Chart	I>WC
•	B3 Practice	Transfer	PW, GW
•	B4 Practice	Transfer/Discussion	GW
•	C1 ▭ Input	Focus Listening/ Information Search	I, PW>WC
•	C2 ▭ Input	Language Chart	I, PW>WC
• •	C3 Practice	Transfer/Writing	PW
(• • •)	Optional exercise 'Newspaper Reporter'	Game	M
•	C4 ▭ Input	Language Chart	PW>WC
•	C5 Practice	Roleplay	PW
•	D1 Input	Reading/Discussion	I>WC
•	D2 Practice	Roleplay	PW
•	D3 Practice	Simulation/Discussion	PW>WC
(• •)	Optional exercises 1 'Three People'	Reading	PW
(• • •)	2 'Feelings'	Role play	PW
• • •	E Thematic Extension	Discussion/Writing	GW
• •	F Learning To Learn	Ranking/Discussion	I>GW>WC

NB See note for Unit 4

Communicative Functions
Expressing feelings
Reacting

Topics and Vocabulary
Gestures
Romantic fiction

Language Focus
Adjective formation : ing/ed
Question tags

Expressing emotions is often complicated involving both linguistic and para-linguistic skills. This unit helps students develop the necessary techniques to communicate and express feelings.

Materials to photocopy: optional exercises 'Animal Noises' vocabulary for A2 'Newspaper Reporter' game for C3 'Three People' reading for D3 'Feelings' roleplay for D3

Materials to collect: none

Alternative Entry Points: D3, E.

A

DESCRIBING FEELINGS

1 Individual/pair work. The extract is an example of romantic fiction or love story. Characters: she feels irritated (frown – 'where have you been?'); impatient (tapping her foot – picture shows her looking at her watch); and then incredulous ('you mean . . . ?' she gasped) and ecstatic (she didn't know whether to laugh or cry). He is happy, rather pleased with himself and confident ('Oh dear!' he thought, 'Now she's in a bad mood! But he smiled . . .)

This exercise can produce a variety of possible alternative answers which can then be discussed by the whole class. Missing words might be: a ring/'Will you marry me?'

2 Pair work. Possible answers:
1 Sally was bored.
2 Dipak was puzzled.
3 Janet was angry.
4 Jill was embarassed/angry.
5 Stan was surprised.
6 Susan was frightened.
7 Dina was upset.
8 Margaret was worried.
9 Lucy was pleased.
10 Walter was angry.
11 Alison was upset/miserable.
12 The dog was pleased.

3 Group work > whole class. This exercise is an opportunity to discuss the use of gestures in different cultures.

Optional exercises
1 Extending from 'gasped' 'sighed', etc. in A1 one could continue the theme of meaningful noises, e.g. puff, pant, snore, sniff, whistle, cough, hum, etc. Working in groups of 3 or 4 ask each group to choose 5 noises and put them together to make a sketch or story.

2 'Animal Noises' see page 88. Pair work.
Answers:
1 a dog: yelp, whimper, yap, bark
  b lion: roar, bellow
  c owl: hoot
  d cat: hiss, purr
  e bull: bellow
  f pig: squeal
  g monkey: chatter
  h bird: chatter, chirp, twitter
  i snake: hiss
  j hen: cackle

2

	with laughter	in anger	in derision	with pain	with delight	in disgust
roar	✓	✓				✓
snort	✓		✓			✓
cackle	✓					
hoot	✓		✓			
squeal	✓			✓	✓	
whimper				✓		
bellow	✓	✓		✓		
yelp				✓		
purr					✓	

3 a barked b chattered c hissed d chirped e yap
4 a camel b bee/wasp c crow d horse
  e wasp/bee/fly
He has the hump today = He's in a bad mood

B

BEING SYMPATHETIC

1 🔊 Individual, pair work > whole class

Conversation 1
Sam You look pleased with yourself!
Dick Yes, I am.
Sam Why's that? What's happened?
Dick You'll never guess! I've won a photographic competition!
Sam Really? [Yeah] That's fantastic! Well done!
Dick Thanks. And erm guess what the prize is?
Sam No, what is it?
Dick I'm going to China for six months as a photographer for a wildlife expedition!
Sam Oh incredible! How exciting!
Dick Yes, I am rather pleased.
Sam Pleased! I'd be absolutely thrilled!

Conversation 2
Sam Hah! You look a bit sorry for yourself.
Dick Yes, I am a bit fed up.
Sam Why? What's the matter?
Dick Oh nothing much. It's just that the trip to China has been cancelled.
Sam Oh no! [Mm] Really? Oh how disappointing for you.
Dick And not only that, I had to give up my job to go there.
Sam Of course you did. Oh that's awful!
Dick Yes, I am rather depressed about it.
Sam Oh I'm sure you are. Cor I would be too.

Conversation 1
Dick feels pleased because he has won a photo competition.
Sam feels envious because he'd like to go to China.

Conversation 2
Dick feels depressed because his trip has been cancelled and he had given up his job.
Sam feels sympathetic because he understands how disappointed Dick is.

2 Individual > whole class

What is exciting? The trip to China.
Who is excited? Dick.
What is disappointing? The trip has been cancelled.
Who is disappointed? Dick.

Possible words for the table:

bored – boring
tired – tiring
interested – interesting, etc.

3
Pair work/small groups. Sam would be thrilled if he was going to China. He is not thrilled now.

4
Group work

C
EXPRESSING YOUR FEELINGS

1 Individual, pair work > whole class

Conversation 1
A Oi! You'll never guess what's happened!
B No, what?
A The woman next door has run off with the postman!
B She hasn't has she? [*laughter*] I don't believe it! [*laughter*]

Conversation 2
A Oh, dear, I'm sure it's going to crash.
B Don't worry, madam. It's quite safe these days, you know. Now please fasten your seatbelt.
A Oh!

Conversation 3
A Hm, I don't think much of this.
B No, mine's pretty awful too.
C Are you enjoying it, sir? Madam?
A Oh, oh it's lovely. Thank you.

Conversation 4
A I'm sorry to hear about your father.
B Thank you. He was very ill, but it's still a shock when it happens.
A Yes, I'm sure it is.

Conversation 5
A Excuse me, I hope you don't mind me asking, but . . .
B No, no, no not at all. What is it?
A Well, erm I don't really know how to put it but erm do you usually wear slippers or shoes for work?
B Shoes of course. Why do you ask?
A It's just that there's a woman on the platform. She seems to be waving at you and she's holding a pair of shoes.
B Oh no!

Conversation 6
A It's going to be marvellous.
B Oh yeah, I'm really looking forward to it.
A She'll look so fantastic in white.
B Oh yes! I can't wait to see her!
A I hope it's sunny for them.
B I'm sure it'll be perfect.

Conversation 7
A What time do you call this?
B Well . . . erm . . .
A I've warned you about this before!
B Yes, but it's so stupid! None of my friends (have to . . .
A That's enough! Upstairs!

Possible answers:

Conversation 1
1 neighbours 2 in a pub 3 surprise/incredulity

Conversation 2
1 passenger and stewardess 2 on a plane 3 fear and reassurance

Conversation 3
1 a couple 2 in a restaurant
3 complaining (to each other) satisfaction (to the waiter)

Conversation 4
1 friends 2 the father of one of them has recently died
3 sympathy/condolence

Conversation 5
1 strangers 2 in a railway carriage 3 embarrassment and irritability

Conversation 6
1 friends **2** anticipating a wedding
3 anticipation/pleasure

Conversation 7
1 father and son **2** son comes home late
3 anger and victimization

These extracts are a good opportunity to highlight the importance of intonation. The tapescript could be reproduced on the blackboard/overhead projector and practiced with different intonations to show the varying interpretations possible. For additional practice see Resource Book B1.

2 Possible answers:

You'll never believe this!	No!
Guess what?	You're joking!
Have you heard the latest news . . . ?	Surely not!

For additional practice/ideas see Resource Book B4. This is also an opportunity to practice the form, different intonation patterns and meanings of Question Tags in English.

3
Pairs. Use your own source of headlines if possible. Students could also invent their own topics, e.g. school or class gossip.

Optional exercise

'Newspaper Reporter' page 88. Melée. Give each student one item of news. Tell them to decide exactly what the headline means – what are the details of the story? The students then need a pad and pencil. They are newspaper reporters and must find out as much news as possible. They must also tell their news when asked and respond appropriately to the news they are told.

At the end of the melée see how much the students have found out. They could write up their news items for homework or find out real-life surprising news and bring the newspaper cuttings to class.

4 Pair work. Possible answers:

Opening
Excuse me, I hope you don't mind my | saying this but . . .
telling you this but . . .
I hope I'm not disturbing you but . . .

Positive reply
No, of course not.
Go ahead.
What is it?

Negative reply
I'm afraid I do mind actually.
I'm afraid you are disturbing me really.

5 Pair work

D

FRIEND OR FOE?

1
Individual > whole class. Possible alternatives:

Complaining to a stranger:
'Could you possibly stop that noise? It's rather annoying'

Reacting to a complaint:
'I'm awfully sorry. I didn't realize . . .'

Complaining to a friend:
'Stop doing that!'
'I've had enough of it!'
'I'm sick of it!'

Reacting to a complaint:
'There's no need to shout!'
'Don't be like that!'
'Don't talk to me like that!'
'Why should I?'
'Oh all right if you insist.'

2 Pair work

3
Pair work > whole class. Useful to discuss appropriate language. Emphasize that it is not only the relationships between the people that govern the choice of language but also the nature of the information, e.g. in 3 the urgency of the situation would allow the use of less polite language. The personality of the speakers also influences the choice of language.

Optional exercise

1 'Three People' on page 89. Reading. Pair work.

2 'Feelings' on pages 90–93. Roleplay. Pair work. Pairs can work on one situation each, or, for more advanced classes, through all nine situations.

Copy the sheets and give each pair Student A and Student B. Cut them into separate cards if you don't want the students to work on all nine situations. Each student should express him/herself according to the emotion given and complete the sentences.

Partners should then guess which emotion is being expressed.

Students should be encouraged to choose and discuss exponents from those already studied. This exercise could be an alternative entry point for diagnostic purposes.

For practice of feelings in Reported Speech see Resource Book B3.

E

THEMES

Small groups. Vocabulary extension. Brainstorm words for each theme, e.g. give students one minute to write down as many words as possible associated with 'Creepy'. Exchange words and (possibly) categorize.

Poems could possibly be written up as on page 64 of Review Unit 3.

F

LEARNING TO LEARN

1   Individual > group work. This discussion should help students become more aware of both the different classroom techniques and the differing preferences within the group, hopefully leading to greater tolerance.

2   This not only gives students a chance to air their misgivings about classroom techniques, but can also be the means of introducing (from fellow students or the teacher) the following ideas:
- Roleplays help you to practise language you wouldn't normally use in the classroom.
- Pair work or group work gives you maximum practice in using the language.
- A large proportion of people in the world are speaking English to other non-native speakers of English.
- (problems in 6) Group work implies co-operation and sensitivity.

REVIEW

UNIT 3

	Approx. Timing	Section	Exercise Type	Classroom Organization
Part 1 Language Review	●	A1 🎧 Cultural Input	Focus Listening/ Information Search	I, PW>WC
	● ●	A2 Cultural Input	Chart/Discussion	I, PW>WC
	●	B1 Cultural Input	Discussion	WC
	● ●	B2 Practice	Reading/Highlighting	I>WC
	● ●	B3 Practice	Roleplay	HH
	●	C1 🎧 Input/Practice	Focus Listening/Highlighting	I, PW>WC
	●	C2 Practice	Discussion	GW, WC
	●	D1 🎧 Input/Practice	Focus Listening/Highlighting	I, PW>WC
	●	D2 Practice	Discussion	I, PW>WC
	●	E1 Vocabulary	Discussion	I>GW, WC
	● ● ●	E2 Practice	Creative Writing	GW>WC
	● ●	F Learning To Learn	Grading	I>GW, WC
Part 2 Simulation	●	A1 Thematic Input	Chart	GW
	●	A2 Thematic Input	Discussion	GW>WC
	● ●	A3 Thematic Input	Discussion	GW
	●	B1 Preparation	Information Search (Map)	I>WC
	● ● ●	B2 Preparation	Reading/Jigsaw Information Search	GW
	● ●	B3 Preparation	Discussion	GW, WC
	●●●●●●●●	C Practice	Simulation	GW

Topics and Vocabulary
The British education system
The Open University

Simulation
Kelapia

The purpose of this unit, apart from revising the language of the previous units, is to discuss the British education system and compare students' own systems.

Materials to photocopy: none
Materials to collect: any pamphlets/information about the Open University
Alternative Entry Points: any section of the Language Review Section Simulation

PART ONE

LANGUAGE REVIEW

A

PATHWAYS

1 🔊 Individual, pair work > whole class. Answers:
1 primary school **3** secondary school
2 primary school **4** technical college

Angi Gary, you're last year in the primary school, aren't you? Erm, tell me about your primary school, you know all the bits of it now, don't you?

Gary Yes, well it's changed a bit because we've got a ne . . new headmaster who's come into the school and he's changed the school. He's made it a bit better for me because I used to be in a very hard class for me, and now I've moved into an easier class which will help me more, I think. Erm, well, it's just one of those primary schools really . . . (ex)cept it might be a little bit smaller. There's five classes. The class that I'm in is just two beach huts put together, just made up this year, this term. Erm, I . . I do quite a lot of subjects. I do English, maths, science, history – things like that – PE, football – just normal things. Erm . . . well, that's about it – quite big playground, erm . . . dunno really, It's just one of those primary schools.

Angi You're a first year what? First year at the primary school?

Jeff Yes.

Angi Aren't you a first year Junior?

Jeff Yeah, I'm a first year Junior, [Ah] at the primary school.

Angi What sort of school is it exactly that you go to?

Lara Just a normal secondary school. It's got a grammar stream in it though. It's either 'O' level or CSE.

Angi All right, Tor, you're at college, aren't you, at the technical college? Can you tell me what subjects you're doing and what the technical college is and where it fits in in the British education system?

Tor Basically the technical college is for people who fall out of the normal education system. And they pick them up to do their 'O' and 'A' levels. It also provides a technical erm schooling for children who leave after 'O' levels, and it does a . . art foundation courses.

2 Individual > whole class. Ages:

Left hand column   **Right hand column**
3–5 (possibly younger) 3–5 (possibly younger)
5–7   6–8
8–11   8–13
11–16   13–16/18
16–18
18+

When discussing their own systems, encourage the students to draw diagrams to illustrate them. Diagrams (perhaps put up around the room if a mixed nationality class) are a useful method for making comparisons leading on to extra writing, for example.

B

THE OPEN UNIVERSITY

1 Whole class. The Open University was first conceived in 1963 as a 'University of the Open Air' and was finally born in 1971 when it received its Royal Charter. Since then it has become a national institution and an established part of today's university life. (In 1987, 82,251 people, including a barmaid, a postman, a lighthouse keeper and a professional footballer were awarded degrees!)

How is the Open University different?

The Open University broke all conventions by not insisting on formal academic qualifications for its degree courses.

Students do not attend a campus but learn at home in their own time. Specially written booklets (course units), together with recommended textbooks, radio and TV broadcasts and other audio-visual material form the core materials. Students may also have home kits for do-it-yourself experiments.

There is face-to-face tuition at regional study centres and annual residential summer schools are held at various universities.

Students wishing to qualify for a BA must successfully complete a number of course 'credits' over a period of years (6 credits for an ordinary degree; 8 for an honours degree).

A full credit course takes an average 12–14 hours study each week for a period of 32 weeks. Students can take a maximum of 2 full credits a year so the shortest time in which they can graduate is 3 years, but the majority complete in 4 to 6 years.

The Open University offers associate student programmes, some 200 packs and courses on a wide range of subjects, particularly Continuing Education courses, Personal Interest Packs and Community Education Packs. The Open University is financed largely by the government and student fees (1987: £158 for a full credit and £79 for a half credit).

Further information from: The Open University Public Relations Department, Walton Hall, Milton Keynes MK7 6AA.

2 Individual > whole class. Advice from Viv:
1 check own motivation and alternative full-time courses
2 be domestically organized/disciplined
3 get support from spouse/partner
4 get a video recorder/radio cassette
5 attend tutorials if possible
6 organize to get away to the Summer School
7 do a foundation course to begin with

Viv thinks the Open University is a good thing but has some reservations. It's a bit solitary, takes a long time, etc.

3 Half/half

C

WHAT SHOULD I DO?

1 Individual, pair work > whole class

Angi Now then, if if . . . You remember Russell's little sister?
Jeff Yes.
Angi And before she, she's only just started school, hasn't she? [Yes] What erm . . . did you give her some advice and tell her things that she should or shouldn't do at school?
Jeff No, not particularly. I've told a f . . f few people called Gareth and Jamie Murdock not to copy a rude boy at school called Campbell, [Mm] he normally tells them rude words. [Mm] But I try not to.
Angi Yes, so you think erm new children shouldn't copy rude words?
Jeff Yes [OK] 'cause it's not nice. [Right]
Angi Anything else?
Jeff Erm . . . yes, you mustn't jump over the walls and stand on the wall or climb the fence [Mm] or fight.
Angi You aren't allowed to fight?

Jeff No. [Oh] And . . . erm . . . and we we on Wednesdays we have music. And we sing with the headmaster and some . . and he takes his guitar in.
Angi What about Gary, here? He might be coming to your school next year. Erm have you got any advice for him? Can you tell him some things he should know?
Lara He should work hard before he gets to the fourth year, 'cause that's when it gets too late, and then you suddenly realize that you should work again, and (a) lot of people make that mistake.
Angi Yes, anything about the discipline of the school or how it works?
Lara Erm (it) just works like a normal school. I can't say much about it.
Angi OK. Thanks.

Angi Erm if you . . . if you erm had to recommend the school or had to tell a a new child about the school, what would you say?
Gary Same thing as Jeffrey, really.

Tor People coming straight from school, I'd say forget all about teachers and the normal things you've been used to and the discipline and s . . try and discipline yourself, really because that's what it's all about. No teacher's going to force you into doing anything really. You're going to have to use your own motivation. I'd take that into consideration.

Answers:
Lara says the most important thing is to work hard before getting into the fourth year. Tor says you have to use your own motivation.

Jeff advises children not to copy rude words; jump over the wall; stand on the wall. Gary agrees with him.

Lara says the discipline at her school works like any other school. Tor says to forget all the normal things you're used to and just discipline yourself.

2 Discussion

D

OPINIONS ABOUT SCHOOL

1 Individual, pair work > whole class. Only Lara is not enthusiastic about school.

Angi OK, why do you find it so boring?
Lara Because the lessons aren't made interesting enough. It's so boring. It's the same routine all the time.
Angi So, it's the routine that you don't like? W . . what does the day, school day go like, then?

Lara Get up in the morning at eight o'clock, get dressed, eat breakfast, walk to school, go to loads of lessons, come home again, go to sleep.
Angi Ah ha. That sounds boring put like that. What lessons do you do?
Lara Erm geography, English, French, maths, PE, cookery, art, that's it.
Angi Well, to me that sounds quite interesting. Why don't you like the lessons?
Lara I don't know. I think it's the teachers most of the time. [Mm] They bore me.
Angi How could they be better?
Lara Erm, I think if we did more practical work, more than doing notes and just writing things down all the time 'cause it gets boring.
Angi So what do you think of the tech., then?
Tor I think it's quite a good place. It's erm, a melting pot for all sorts of races and ages, it's erm it's got people of different academic levels. I mean there's real under-achievers there who do, erm erm an OND in woodwork or something like that. There again it's got people who are doing post 'A' level courses. Erm an architect . . architects and people on HND catering degrees, which is . . if they come out with a first from that they're obviously going to high places. Coming from school as a . . I don't know of personal experience coming, what coming from school's like, but I would imagine that the freedom that you get at college compared to school is quite enjoyable. People who can smoke, can erm go downtown at lunchtimes, can go home can take the afternoon off if they haven't got any lessons. There's a wide range of erm activities to do, a hundred or so clubs. Erm, then there's the CAP system which gives you a choice of electives to take up – pottery, acting – anything from erm, from sewing classes to rebuilding a car.
Angi What do you think of it? What do you think of the school? What do you think of the teachers?
Gary Well, the school's OK, I would say, but the teachers, well, they're quite good, but I reckon they could be a bit more . . . not so strict really. Some of them are OK, but some of them push a lot.
Angi Push a lot, what do you mean?
Gary . . . In some ways it's good, but . . . I don't like it much.
Angi OK. What's your favourite subject?
Gary Erm, (I) haven't really got a favourite subject – sport and play really – out . . . just missing out science, I mean missing out PE and football and things like that. I think science . . . the interesting . . . the one that interests me the most.
Angi What do you like about school? Do you like school?
Jeff Yes, I do. It's OK. Erm, I've got I've got a best friend he's he's called Russell. (He) I always meet him in the playground a . . at school and after school. And before we always play together, sometimes, except for erm lunchtimes. Sometimes I play chess. And . . and . . and today I beat Timel in chess – that's one of my friends.

2 Individual, pairs > whole class. The statements only refer to general attitudes to school.
1 Jeff **2** Gary **3** Tor **4** Lara

E

FEELINGS ABOUT SCHOOL

1 Individual > group work > whole class. Discussion/vocabulary extension. Encourage precise use of adjectives, not just 'boring', 'nice', etc. Exchange lists in pairs and discuss the intentions behind each list. This may lead to active story telling about episodes at school.

2 Group work

F

LEARNING TO LEARN

Encourage the students to look at how they have assessed themselves and, for items not graded 'very well', ask them to decide if they want to know the item any better. If they do, suggest that they work out for themselves the best way of doing that. The Resource Book, if it has not already been used, may be useful here.

PART TWO
SIMULATION

A
DEVELOPED AND DEVELOPING COUNTRIES

1 Group work. Students to decide whether a country is developed or not. Continents are South America, Australasia, Africa and Asia.

2 Useful to do individual > small groups > whole class. Answers depend on students' opinions.

3 Small groups

B
KELAPIA

1 Individual > whole class. Resources are: (good) beaches; iron ore; reasonable communications; areas of outstanding beauty, etc.

2 Group work. Class of 10 could read extracts in pairs to make it quicker. Then redivide into groups of five to discuss answers.
1 900 miles off the coast of Africa in the Indian Ocean
2 There was a military coup
3 Kelawi, African, Indian, Mixed, Others
4 Protestant
5 Plantation agriculture

It is essential that students are clear on this background before proceeding on to the simulation. (The reading could possibly also be done as individual homework.)

3
1 Climate, good beaches, etc.
2 This question highlights the problem that developing countries have faced with a sudden tourist boom. Encourage students to look carefully at the tables of statistics and discuss the positive/negative effects of the tourist boom.

C
THE FUTURE OF KELAPIA

Small groups. There are two possibilities here: either each group could focus on one of the four alternatives and then discuss the issues with the whole class. Or each group could debate all four issues. Encourage students to offer suggestions/alternatives themselves rather than depend only on the four alternatives presented. Remind them to refer to the map and previous information when making/deciding on their proposals.

UNIT 10

Approx. Timing	Section	Exercise Type	Classroom Organization
●	A1 Input	Focus Listening/ Information Search	I, PW>WC
● ●	A2 Input	Chart	PW, GW, WC
● ●	A3 Practice	Roleplay	HH
●	A4 Practice	Discussion/Transfer	PW
●	B1 Practice	Discussion	I>GW
● ●	B2 Reading	Discussion	GW
●	B3 Practice	Discussion	PW, GW
●	C1 Input	Discussion	GW
● ●	C2 Practice	Maze Reading	GW
●	D1 Cultural Input	Reading/Information Search	I, PW>WC
● ●	D2 Reading	Discussion	I, PW>GW
(● ●) (● ● ● ●)	Optional exercises End of 'The First Men' and/or 'True Love' a sci-fi short story	Reading	I
●	D3 Thematic extension	Ranking/Discussion	I>GW>WC
● ●	E Learning To Learn	Discussion	GW>WC

Communicative Functions
Expressing certainty and uncertainty
Speculating about the future

Topics and Vocabulary
Science fiction

Language Focus
1st and 2nd Conditionals

The purpose of this unit is to encourage students to develop their imagination — a powerful capacity of the brain — often neglected, but which can provide a useful spur to further learning.

Materials to photocopy: optional exercises: 'The First Men' for D2
'True Love' a short story for D2

Materials to collect: none

Alternative Entry Points: B, D, E

A

POSSIBILITIES

1 🔲 Individual, pair work > whole class.

Friend What'll you do if you can't find a job in the summer, do you think?
Dominique I don't know, <u>I suppose I'll</u> have to go back to France and try and find a job there.
Friend Mmm . . . What are the possibilities of things you might do in England?
Dominique Oh, work on the beach. I'm waiting to hear about working on the beach, looking after pedaloes. [Oh] Or <u>perhaps I could</u> find a job in a hotel or at the tech.
Friend Well, how will you feel then, John, if Domy doesn't stay in the summer?
John No comment on that. You can't ask me that! If Domy doesn't stay in the summer? That's fine with me, 'cause I'm going to France! [*laughter*]
Friend Supposing you don't find any of those jobs, then what?
Dominique Oh <u>maybe I'll</u> find a job as an au pair, or babysitting, or I don't know.
Friend Yeah. Have you thought of anything else?
Dominique Not really.
Friend Well, how do you think your parents will feel if you don't go home in the summer?
Dominique Upset, I suppose, because they're afraid I'll stay in England. They'll think I'm not coming back!
Friend So, assuming you do find a job in the summer, how long will you stay, do you think?
Dominique I want a job for two months, July and August, and then I have to do a period of training in a firm somewhere around here. If I find a job for longer, then <u>I'll</u> stay longer – until Christmas about. After that I have to go back to France. [Oh]

Answers:
1 work on the beach; job in a hotel; job at the tech.; au pair; babysitting
2 they'll be afraid she'll stay in England
3 until Christmas
4 'I suppose I'll' and 'I'll'. In addition she uses 'Maybe I'll' and 'Perhaps I could'.

2 Pair work

certainty	possibility	perhaps	uncertainty	definitely not
I'll stay . . .	I'll probably stay . . .	Maybe I'll stay . . .	I suppose I could stay . . .	I definitely won't stay . . .
	I think I'll stay . . .	I might possibly stay . . .	I doubt if I'll stay . . .	I'm sure I won't stay . . .
	I expect I'll stay . . .		I probably won't stay . . .	
			I don't think I'll stay . . .	

3 Half/half. Allow enough time for the two groups to prepare ideas as there are no role cards to assist them.

4 Pair work. For further practice of exponents expressing future possibilities see Resource Book B1 and B2.

B

SPECULATION

1 Individual > group. If I had . . . I would . . . etc.

2 Group work. Discussion.

3 Pairs, small groups. This exercise is both for practice of this form and awareness-raising. For further practice of 2nd Conditional and vocabulary see Resource Book B3.

C

IMAGINATION

1 Group work. In order to stimumate the imaginations of the students use any relaxation exercise/technique before starting the exercise and encourage students to focus on all five senses, e.g. City under the sea – How do you feel? What sound do you hear? How are they different? Try to find accurate words to describe your feelings/senses. The language point (2nd conditional) should then be more productive/creative/interesting!

2 Small groups. Encourage discussion between each decision and discourage wanting to get to the end (no 10)!

D

SCIENCE FICTION

1 Individual, pair work > whole class

2 Individual, pair work > discussion after extract A > group work after extract B.

Answers:

Extract A – They can communicate without speaking. This could lead to discussion as to what extent language is important in communication.

Extract B – The children are a danger to the outside world because of this power.

The story ends with the children making the reservation disappear into the future. When the government realizes what the children have done they make the arrangements to conduct the scientific research necessary to find and ultimately kill them, as the children predicted.

Optional exercises
The end of 'The First Men' on page 93, and/or a short sci-fi story 'True Love' page 94. Reading.

3 Individual > group work. This could be a pyramid discussion activity – students make their own ranking then compare with a partner then two pairs compare together then each group reports to the whole class.

E

LEARNING TO LEARN

This discussion could lead to the conclusion that the teacher can't 'learn' for the students she/he can only try to help the students to learn. What is more, if students take responsibility for their own learning and participate actively in class they will not only be able to learn more but will enjoy the process.

UNIT 11

Approx. Timing	Section	Exercise Type	Classroom Organization
●	A1 Input	Discussion	PW>WC
● ●	A2 Practice	Discussion	GW
(● ●)	Optional exercises 'Who is Dave?'	Information Search	GW
(● ●)	'Problem solving puzzles'		GW, WC
●	B1 Input	Discussion	PW>WC
● ●	B2 Practice	Discussion	PW>WC
● ● ●	Optional exercise 'Black Horse Murder'	Game	M
●	C1 Practice	Focus Listening	I>WC
● ●	C2 Practice	Discussion	PW>WC
●	D1 Reading	Information Search	I>GW
● ● ●	D2 Jigsaw	Information Gap	GW>WC
● ●	D3 Practice	Discussion	GW
(● ● ● ● ● ●)	Optional extra 'Tribes'	Simulation/Game	HH
● ●	E Learning To Learn	Discussion	I>GW, WC

Communicative Functions
Deducing
Speculating

Topics and Vocabulary
Museum pieces
Mysteries: The Bermuda Triangle

Language Focus
Modals: can/can't could/couldn't must/might

The purpose of this unit is to use the language of deduction and speculating in a stimulating way.

Materials to photocopy: optional exercise: 'Who is Dave?' after A2
optional exercise: Melée game 'The Black Horse Murder' after B
optional exercise: Game/simulation 'Tribes' after D

Materials to collect: optional: problem solving puzzles for A
optional: any unusual objects/photos, etc.
optional: any books/articles referring to unsolved mysteries
optional: props for 'Tribes'

Alternative Entry Points: D, E.

A

WHO OR WHAT CAN IT BE?

1 Pair work. Ask the students to cover up the clues and put a blank chart on the blackboard/overhead projector. Then give the clues one by one and elicit the language.

2 Group work. Answers:
1 Pen
2 Spiral-bound book
3 Tennis racket
4 Bar of chocolate
5 Cassette
6 Plug
7 Ball of string
8 Top of a tube of toothpaste
9 Ring-pull can

For further practice on Present Deductions see Resource Book B1, B2 and B3.

Alternatively, use any lateral thinking/problem solving puzzles you may have/know for further practice.

Optional exercise
'Who is Dave?' Information search. Group work. See page 95.

B

WHO OR WHAT CAN IT HAVE BEEN?

1 As in A1.

2 Pair work. Encourage students to think of original but still logical deductions. Compare with others. For further practice on Past Deductions see Resource Book B4 and B5.

Alternatively, use any lateral thinking/problem solving puzzles you may know/have, e.g.
a Two Mexicans were walking down the street. One was the father of the other one's son. How could this be? Answer: one is a woman.

b One day a cat fell down a well. The well was eighteen feet deep. When the cat tried to climb out it found that the sides of the well were very damp and slippery. However with patient determination it finally managed to climb out. It took the cat one minute of climbing to gain three feet. But after climbing for a minute the cat had to rest for a minute before it could go on. During each minute of the rest the cat slid back two feet.
How long did it take for the cat to get out of the well?
Answer: 31 minutes.

Optional exercise
'The Black Horse Murder' page 95. Game. Melée.

Rules
1 28 cards. Divide them out among the class if there are 28 or less students.
2 The aim of the game is to find out:
WHO –
TIME –
PLACE –
MOTIVE –
WEAPON –

Write the above list on the blackboard and get the students to work out what happened, i.e. how the story develops from the information given on his/her card. Don't give them any clues! They will soon come up with the order of events.

Answers: WHO – Barton TIME – 10.15 p.m.
PLACE – car park MOTIVE – blackmail WEAPON – spanner

C

MUSEUM PIECES

1 Individual. Answer: picture 2.

Old lady Now, what room is this, Hank?
Hank I'm not sure, something to do with erm household. I think.
Old lady Of course! I remember now. This is the kitchen section. Erm . . . What have we here? . . . Damn! I can't find my glasses. What does the notice say?
Hank Erm . . . I can't see one. It's a little house, made of erm . . . how you say it? . . . Wood.
Old lady Wood, yes. But not a house – it says 'chapel' on the lid. I wonder what it was used for?
Hank Maybe it's a model, to go over the fireplace.
Old lady No, no it couldn't be. At least, it wasn't usual to put models in the kitchen. They went in the parlour, or living room. No, it must be something to do with the kitchen. Perhaps a a container of some sort.

Hank Container?
Old lady Yes, you know . . . for putting things in! [Oh] Maybe it was used for putting biscuits in.
Hank Erm not many biscuits. It's very small.
Old lady Oh you're right. It couldn't have been used for that.
Hank Perhaps it was used for erm tea or coffee or salt?
Old lady Yes, that's what it might have been used for . . . Oh! Oh look! I've found my glasses. And there's the notice, at the side . . . Oh of course . . . Tea! A tea caddy! It was used for keeping tea in, in the time of Queen Victoria. It's very old.

2 Pair work > whole class. Answers:
1 Sugar loaf
2 Tea caddy
3 Tennis ball cleaner
4 Ale warmer

This is an opportunity of either presenting the students with photos of unusual objects or bringing in some actual objects. It might be possible to invite the curator of the local museum to come in and give an illustrated talk, or make a visit to a local museum.

D

THE BERMUDA TRIANGLE

Jigsaw reading exercise. Group work.

1 The students divide into three groups, read about one mystery in each group and answer the questions.

2 They re-form into groups of three people, one from each original group, and tell each other their stories/theories.

3 Discussion
Answers:

Mystery 1
1 true
2 true
3 true
4 false
5 false

Mystery 2
1 boat that pulls other boats
2 instrument for finding directions
3 boat used for carrying heavy loads
4 pull along
5 people who keep a check on the sea and shipping
6 international signal for help
7 undamaged, complete
8 strange

Mystery 3
1 watches were synchronized
2 plane on radar screen
3 plane disappeared
4 crews watches lost 10 minutes
5 plane reappeared on the screen
6 plane landed

Optional exercise
'Tribes' on page 96. Game/simulation. Half/half. With acknowledgements to Tom Hunter.

Warning! This activity works best with groups who know each other well, and are prepared to be quite unconventional!

Two rooms, one for each tribe, are essential for this activity. However, as it can be used with quite large numbers, perhaps two classes could unite. One teacher per tribe saves a lot of leg-work too.

Materials: Copies of 'Tribe Rules' see page 96.
For 'Happy Tribe': big notice of motto *Keep Smiling*, soft music, cushions, scented candles, etc.
For 'Trading Tribe': big notice of motto *Keep Trying*, notice of 'bank rates', i.e. 10 = 100, 5 = 10, pot of 3 sorts of dried foods, e.g. macaroni, beans, split peas.

Method:
1 Explain the simulation – the group is going to 'live' as two different tribes, and they are going to send ambassadors into each other's tribes. They in turn will try to help their tribe work out how the other tribe lives. DO NOT LET ONE TRIBE SEE THE OTHER TRIBE'S RULES.
2 Split class into two groups and allocate rooms.
3 Give out 'Tribe Rules' and help each group rearrange each room and create a suitable atmosphere.
4 Put up notices, allow each group to work out its own rituals/interpretations of rules.
5 Five minutes of strict tribal life, before . . .
6 First exchange of ambassadors (one, two or three volunteers, depending on numbers). Maximum length of visit three minutes, or less if own ambassador returns early.
7 Tribe discussion of the customs/rules of the other tribe based on ambassadors' report.
8 New ambassadors go out, testing hypotheses, reporting back until every member of each tribe has visited the other.
9 Bring the two tribes together and let them check their understanding of tribe rules, comment on their

feelings, etc. Pick up on comments from ambassadors as they returned to their own tribes 'They're crazy in there!', etc. and invite comment. Possible extension into discussion on racial relationships/problems and some of the underlying reasons.

Time: 1–1½ hours.

E
LEARNING TO LEARN

1 Research seems to show that the affective component (how the student feels about learning in general; previous language learning experiences; the present experience; source and strength of motivation; attitudes towards the target language – its culture and people; the teacher) is at least as important if not more so than the cognitive components (general IQ, language aptitude; etc.) in the make up of a successful language learner. The discussion on what constitutes a good teacher should prove useful feedback, although it is our contention that what is true for the student is also true for the teacher/learner.

2 Project work; these Learning To Learn sections; the dictionary work in the Resource Book and other techniques and exercises are there to help students learn how to continue their learning without a teacher or a group.

UNIT 12

Approx. Timing	Section	Exercise Type	Classroom Organization
● ●	A1 Thematic Input	Reading/Information Search	I, PW>WC
●	A2 ▭ Input	Focus Listening/Chart	I, PW>WC
●	A3 Input	Matching	PW
●	A4 Practice	Roleplay	PW
●	B1 Input	Matching	PW>WC
● ●	B2 Practice	Transfer	PW
(● ● ●)	Optional exercise 'To Mary'	Reading/Discussion	PW>WC
● ●	B3 Input/Practice	Transfer	PW
	B4 Practice	Transfer/Discussion	PW, GW
(● ● ● ●)	Optional exercise 'Domestic Bliss'	Reading/Roleplay	HH>PW
● ●	C1 Input	Reading	I>WC
	C2 Practice	Transfer	PW, GW
●	C3 Input	Discussion	PW>WC
●	C4 Practice	Discussion	PW, GW>WC
● ●	D1 ▭ Thematic Input	Focus Listening/ Information Search	I, PW>WC
●	D2 Practice	Discussion	GW, WC
● ●	E Learning To Learn	Discussion	GW>WC

Communicative Functions
Regretting
Wishing and hoping

Topics and Vocabulary
A chapter of accidents
Martin Luther King

Language Focus
3rd Conditional

This unit aims to move from the more negative sentiment of regret to the more optimistic and purposeful area of positive wishes.

Materials to photocopy: optional exercise: 'To Mary'
B2
optional exercise: 'Domestic Bliss' after B

Materials to collect: none
Alternative Entry Points: C, D, E

A

REGRETS

1 Individual, pair work > whole class.
Answers: **1** at least 12 **2** Discussion

2 Individual, pair work > whole class

Interviewer ... So, tell us about this disastrous honeymoon. I erm I gather it all started with the ring?
Dave Yes.
Sandy Yeah, that's right. My finger swelled up so much I had to rip the ring off! [Oh, dear]
Dave Mm, I wish we'd known you were allergic to gold. [Mm] I would've bought you a platinum one. [Yeah]
Interviewer And erm, then what?
Dave [Erm] Well erm, [Oh] then it was the Bank Holiday weekend [Mm] and we couldn't cash our traveller's cheques.
Sandy Yeah, we were stupid, weren't we, to have forgotten that?
Dave Oh yeah, then of course, it was the car ...
Interviewer The car?
Sandy New one! What we'd always dreamt of ...
Dave Yeah, well first it broke down, and the, and the same night it was stolen.
Interviewer Oh dear!
Dave I suppose we should have left it at home really, but erm you see we'd only just got it.
Sandy Yeah, so anyway, w.. we hired another car. Blow me if the clutch didn't go on that too! It cost a lot of money to stay in a hotel. And then, because it was the weekend and we didn't have any money left, we had to drive for oh ... how long? [Six .. sixteen] Sixteen? Yeah sixteen hours back into France. Oh we should never have forgotten the banks again.
Dave Yeah, we must have been crazy to have driven all that way, because it was the last straw for you, because you were ill then.
Sandy Oh yeah, well, it wasn't just that, it was the sun, a .. and the food too.
Dave (Yeah) Suppose so.
Interviewer So erm, you came home then, did you?
Sandy Oh yeah, but at the port someone stole my purse!
Interviewer Oh!
Dave I wish we'd spent that money on duty-frees. [Oh yeah] And then to cap it all when we got home we found our shop had been burgled....
Sandy Oh we found that ... yeah ... yeah!
Interviewer Why on earth didn't you tell the police you were away?
Dave Erm ... I suppose it erm it slipped our minds with the with ...
Sandy Erm ... didn't think ...
Dave ... the wedding and all that ...
Sandy Well, we had a lot to think about ... [Yeah] ...

Things they did	Things they didn't do	Things they blame themselves for
'We must have been crazy to have driven all that way ...' 'It slipped our minds ...'	'I wish we'd known you were allergic to gold ...' 'I would have bought you a platinum one ...' 'I suppose we should have left it at home really ...' 'I wish we'd spent that money on duty-frees ...'	'We were stupid to have forgotten ...' 'We should never have forgotten the banks ...'

3 Pair work. Answers:
1 and **3** = we hadn't taken our car on honeymoon.
2 and **5** = did we take our car on honeymoon?
4   = have taken our car on honeymoon.
6   = have known it was a bank holiday.
7 and **10** = didn't we know it was a bank holiday?
8 and **9** = we had known it was a bank holiday.

4 Pair work. For additional work on the language of Regrets see Resource Book B1.

B

I MUST HAVE BEEN CRAZY ...

1 Pair work. Answers:
1 Perhaps I should have ...
2 I'm beginning to wish I hadn't ...
3 If only I'd ...
4 I simply can't think why I decided ...
5 I must have been crazy ...

2 Pair work.

Optional exercise
'To Mary' on page 97. Reading/Discussion. Pair work > whole class.

The poem could be exploited in a number of ways, e.g. leave gaps for the students to fill in the verbs or 'true' or 'false' questions; discussion on the use of archaic English; what do you think the poet regrets?, etc.

3 Pair work

4 Pair work or small groups

Optional exercise
Roleplay. Half/half. 'Domestic Bliss' page 97. When both groups have decided what they want to say, divide them into pairs, one from each group, to act out their roles.

C

PRESENT WISHES

1 Whole class presentation

2 Pair work, group work. Possible answers:
1 I wish they would leave.
2 I wish I hadn't brought the car/ I wish there was less traffic.
3 I wish the shop was open.

For further work on the language of Wishing see Resource Book B4.

3 Pair work. Possible answers: **1** I hope they go soon **2** I hope the traffic clears soon
3 I hope the shop opens soon, etc.

4 Small groups. Encourage students to elaborate as much as possible.

D

FUTURE HOPES

1 Individual, pair work

[applause] . . . I say to you today, my friends, [applause] so even though we face the difficulties of today and tomorrow, I still have a dream. It is a dream deeply rooted in the American dream. I have a dream that one day this nation will rise up, live out the true meaning of its creed. 'We hold these truths to be self-evident, that all men are created equal.' [applause] I have a dream that one day on the red hills of Georgia, sons of former slaves and the sons of former slave owners will be able to sit down together at the table of brotherhood. I have a dream [applause] that one day, even the state of Mississippi, a state sweltering with the heat of injustice, sweltering with the heat of oppression, be transformed into an oasis of freedom and justice. I have a dream [applause] that my four little children will one day live in a nation where they will not be judged by the colour of their skin, but by the content of their character. [applause] . . .

Four hopes: **1** The nation will recognize and put into practice that all men are created equal. **2** The descendants of former slaves and slave owners will live together as equals. **3** Mississippi will no longer be a state of prejudice and inequalities. **4** His children will live in a nation which judges people by their character, not by the colour of their skin.

Discussion on whether any of his dreams have come true.

2 Small groups. For further practice on Future Hopes see Resource Book B3.

E

LEARNING TO LEARN

1 While working on this course, students will have become a group. From group dynamic studies we have learnt that time must be given to ending the group-life; to working out, whilst still within the group, support systems or ways of pursuing individual goals, if the students are not to feel 'lost' or abandoned. (And the effective responses as a result of the learning experience are also important in the makeup of a successful language learner.)

2 Students often come up with other practical ways of continuing their learning.

REVIEW

UNIT 4

	Approx. Timing	Section	Exercise Type	Classroom Organization
Part 1 Language Review	• •	A Cultural Input	Discussion	GW>WC
	• • •	B1 Cultural Input	Reading/Information Search	PW>WC
	• •	B2 Practice	Focus Listening/Information Search	I>WC
	• •	B3 Practice	Discussion	PW
	•	B4 Practice	Discussion/Roleplay	PW
	• •	C1 Cultural Input	Reading/Listening/Note Taking	I, PW>WC
	•	C2 Practice	Discussion	PW, GW, WC
	• •	D1 Cultural Input	Reading/Information Search	I, PW
	•	D2 Practice	Discussion	GW
	• •	D3 Practice	Discussion	GW>WC
Part 2 Course Review	•	A1 Learning To Learn	Grading	I>WC
	• •	A2 Learning To Learn	Discussion/Writing	I>PW
	• •	A3 Learning To Learn	Discussion	GW>WC
	• •	B Practice	Matching	I,PW>WC
	• • • •	C Practice	Roleplay	PW, GW
	•	D1 Vocabulary	Word Association	I>WC
	•	D2 Listening	Information Search	I>WC
	•	D3 Listening	Gap Fill	I>WC
	•	D4 Vocabulary	Vocabulary Sorting	I>WC
	•	D5 Listening	Jigsaw	I>WC
	• •	D6 Listening	Discussion	I>GW>WC
	(• •)	Optional exercise 'The Leaving of Liverpool' additional exercises	Listening/Information Search	I>WC

Topics and Vocabulary
Ethnic groups in Britain
Carnivals and festivals

Part 2: Course review

The purpose of the unit is to review in Part 1 the language of the previous three units through the topic of ethnic groups in Britain. Part 2 aims both to briefly review the language of the whole course and afford the opportunity for students to take stock of the whole course experience.

Materials to photocopy: optional exercise 'The Leaving of Liverpool' additional exercises for Part 2D on page 97

Materials to collect: none

Alternative Entry Points: Part 1 any section, Part 2B or C

PART ONE

LANGUAGE REVIEW

A

IT MIGHT BE . . .

Group work. Answers:
1 Notting Hill Carnival, London
2 Regents Park Mosque, London
3 Community Development Centre, Cardiff
4 Proposed new Hindu Temple in Brent, London

B

FESTIVALS

1 Pair work. A could read 'Festival of Chinese Culture', B could read 'Notting Hill Carnival' and together work out the answers to the questions.
Answers:
– West Indians predominantly celebrate the Carnival in Notting Hill.
– Activities in the festival of Chinese culture for children could be: face painting, kite flying, story telling, etc.

1 You can listen to music, you can see dancing/costumes.
2 Reggae, brass/steel bands and pop at Notting Hill. In Cardiff, folk music, traditional and modern Chinese music and opera.
3 Discussion.

2 Individual > whole class

Anita Did you get to the carnival on Monday?
Beverly Yeah, but in a way I wished I'd stayed at home. I don't know why I didn't think to dress more suitably.
Anita Yeah, it did rain rather a lot. Was it a complete wash-out?
Beverly Oh no, if only I'd got there earlier I might have found a more sheltered vantage point. I got soaked right at the beginning listening to the calypso. Why ever didn't the organizers think to put up awnings or something?
Anita Well, they weren't to know, were they? Anyway the whole thing's on the move, isn't it?
Beverly Yeah, that's true. I suppose I should at least have thought to take my mac.
Anita Well, these things happen. You don't think, do you?
Beverly No. Anyhow, it was such a pity. The costumes were really gorgeous, they obviously spent a lot of time making them. I bet they wished they were in Trinidad instead of London, don't you?
Anita Yeah, I wouldn't mind being there either! But there were a lot of people there, weren't there?
Beverly Yeah, it didn't seem to dampen enthusiasm really. We all got going with reggae bands, and the steel bands they seemed really inventive this year. Yeah, it was good. Let's just pray for better weather next year.

Beverly regrets: not staying at home (weather); not dressing more suitably; not getting there earlier; not taking her mac (she blames the organizers for not putting up awnings). She most enjoyed the costumes and the steel bands.

3 Pair work

4 Pair work

C

HINDU HOPES

1 Individual, pair work

Arthur Here, have you heard? [What?] They're going to build a new church near Harrow School.
Terry Get away! [Yeah] Nobody goes to church these days. [Yeah] Anyway, who's 'they?'
Arthur I don't know, them erm, Harry Christa lot, I think.
Terry Mm . . . What sort of churches do they have, then?
Arthur Well, I don't know, but I heard it's all going to be erm bronze and erm silver and stuff. Ten million pounds they say it's going to cost!
Terry Sounds like a second Buck House to me. [Yeah] Who's going to cough up, then?
Arthur Search me. Another flag day soon, I suppose.

Answer:
They get five facts wrong. It isn't a church but a temple. It isn't near Harrow School but Northwick Park Hospital (the grounds belong to the school). It isn't the 'Harry Christa lot' but the Hindus who are building it. It is going to be built with marble and gold not bronze and silver. The estimated cost is £5 million not £10 million.

2 Pair work, small groups

D
WORDS OF COMFORT

1 Individual, pair work. Particular problems are associated with having a baby in a foreign country where you don't speak the language, and without the support of the extended family.

2 Small group discussion. Students may be able to give additional examples of problems encountered in a country where you do not speak the language well.

3 Small group > whole class

PART TWO
COURSE REVIEW

A
ASSESSMENT

1 Individual > whole class

2 Individual > pair work. See notes Unit 12 E.

3 Group work. See notes Unit 12 E.

B
LANGUAGE REVIEW

Individual, pair work > whole class.

Answers:
1. Don't know really.
2. How do you do?
3. Sorry, I'm a stranger here myself.
4. Why don't you sleep on it?
5. A Scotch and soda please.
6. Yes, of course.
7. What a good idea!
8. You weren't to know, were you?
9. I'm sorry sir, would you like to exchange it?
10. The USA does.
11. I'd feel very excited.
12. I expect I'll take them again.
13. It must be Fred.

Students could choose one of the above exchanges and extend the dialogue giving it context and characters, etc. and act their sketch to another pair or the whole class.

C
LAST LINES

Pairs, small groups

D
THE LEAVING OF LIVERPOOL

1 Individual > whole class

2 *The Leaving of Liverpool*

Fare thee well the Prince's Landing Stage.
River Mersey, fare thee well.
For I'm bound for Californiay
A place that I know right well.

Chorus
<u>So</u> fare thee well, my <u>own</u> true <u>love</u>.
When I <u>return</u> <u>united</u> we <u>will</u> be.
It's <u>not</u> the <u>leaving</u> of Liverpool <u>that</u> grieves <u>me</u>,
But, me <u>darling</u>, when I <u>think</u> of thee.

Yes, I'm bound for California
By way of the stormy Cape Horn.
But you know I'll write to you a letter,
Me love, when I'm homeward bound.

Repeat chorus
I have shipped on a Yankee clipper ship
Davy Crockett is her name.
And her captain's name it is Burgess,
And they say she's a floating shame.

Repeat chorus
Oh the tug is a waiting at the pier head
To take us down the stream.
Our sails are loose and the anchor is stowed
So fare thee well again.

Repeat chorus
Fare thee well to Lower Frederick Street,
Anson Terrace and Ole Parkee Lane.
For I know that it's going to be a long, long time
Before I see you again.

Repeat chorus twice

Answers:
river = Mersey   ship = Davy Crockett
destination = California   captain = Burgess
town = Liverpool

3 Individual. See tapescript. 'Grieves me' = causes me deep suffering

4 'Fare thee well' = goodbye; 'Bound for' = going to

5 See tapescript

6 Discussion.

Optional exercise
Additional exercises for the song on page 97.

OPTIONAL EXERCISES

The optional exercises, games and role cards in the following pages are to be photocopied, in some cases cut up, and distributed to the students.

Each exercise is cross-referenced to the Section and the Unit with which it can be used. Instructions to the student are given where appropriate; other instructions, including all instructions to the teacher, are given under the relevant Section and Unit in the main Teachers' Notes.

Who Am I? ✂ for use with Section A1, Introductory Unit

Fill in the spaces with information about yourself.

I hate . . .

I like . . .

I have . . .

I am good at . . .

I am bad at . . .

Fold the piece of paper and give it to your teacher. Your teacher will shuffle the papers and give you a new one. Your job is to find the person whose piece of paper you have. Ask questions with:
'Do you . . .?'
'Are you . . .?'
'Have you ever . . .?'

Job Cards ✂ for use with Section D1, Introductory Unit

	Job C	Job D
Wages/Salary Hours Holiday Qualifications Travel to work Length of journey Start work Finish work Like Dislike		

Job C

Farmworker

George Davey, 39, is a labourer on a lowland Devon farm near Cheriton Bishop. He drives the five miles from the house he owns in Crediton where he lives with his wife and two young children. The farm is 325 acres, devoted to sheep (350 breeding ewes) and arable — plus about 30 chickens. As the only full-time employee (contract labour is used when needed) George does general chores and looks after the care and breeding of the sheep with the help of two collies. He buys feed, runs the animals through the bath, worms and marks them and is responsible for grass management.
EARNINGS £346 gross a month (£4,152 a year basic; variable overtime can add another £500 a year). PERKS Right to grow his own potatoes and peas on the farm (uses land for nothing but buys his own seed and fertiliser). Free eggs.
HOURS In theory a 40-hour week. In practice very flexible hours, not all overtime charged. "You don't watch the clock when you are farming; if something has to be done, you do it." Typical day 8 a.m. to 6 p.m. Perhaps six hours over the weekend. In lambing season, with 350 ewes producing, there are 800–900 sheep to look after so he sleeps at the farm lodge, and works a 15- to 18-hour day. Holiday: three weeks.
CONDITIONS Gets around the farm mainly on foot but uses the tractor when feeding the sheep. They graze most of the time but in winter get hay and concentrates. Arable side is largely mechanized and much routine work is handled by contract labour. Out in all weathers.
TRAINING Left school at 15, without qualifications. Could not get the carpentry apprenticeship he wanted so did various jobs — worked in a laundry (four months) and in a market garden (12 months). Worked for five years on a small mixed farm (sheep, corn, and a few cows). Spent two years on a building site, then did relief farm labouring until present job.
PROSPECTS "Can't get much higher without owning my own farm. It would be my dream but money is the problem. Even if you rent the land, you need capital to stock it." Some labourers on larger farms eventually become managers.
JOB SECURITY Good. Notice: six months.
DRAWBACKS "You never know what time you will be home."
ATTRACTIONS "The open air, the countryside and the variety in farming."

Job D

Public relations executive

Jane Fox, 29, is an account director with a leading public relations agency, Burson-Marsteller. She is unmarried and when in England lives in Ealing, a 30–40 minute drive from her office in the West End of London. One of about 50 executives, she is in charge of four accounts — for chemical, lingerie, watch and electronics companies. She helps them "project company image", handle the press and get publicity on radio and television.
EARNINGS £21,300 gross, plus annual bonus (dependent on firm's profit and personal performance). PERKS Car. BUPA cover. Some business lunches. Occasional travel, and foreign postings (she is currently in Geneva).
HOURS Officially 35 hours a week, in practice much longer. Holiday: four weeks.
CONDITIONS Office functional rather than glamourous. High-pressure job with constant deadlines and quick decisions needed.
TRAINING English degree from Oxford. Press officer at Design Council for two-and-a-half years. At Burson-Marsteller training is continual with constant refresher courses.
PROSPECTS Eventual possibility of seat on the Board. Alternatively could transfer to industry and join a firm as a senior executive.
JOB SECURITY The recession has contracted the public relations world, though experienced and valued personnel are unlikely to be vulnerable. Notice: three months.
DRAWBACKS "You can't afford to have off days as there is a sense of performance about the job and as relationships with clients and colleagues are paramount." Difficult to switch off: "even at weekends you find yourself thinking about work."
ATTRACTIONS Immense variety. "Both the job and the people I meet are very stimulating."

Earning A Living

for use with Section D3, Introductory Unit

Complete this questionnaire about your work (or a job you would like to do).

	You	Your partner
What do you do?		
Where do you work?		
How long have you worked there?		
How much do you earn?		
How many hours do you work?		
When do you start work?		
When do you finish work?		
What qualifications have you got?		
What position do you hold?		
Why did you choose your job?		
What are the prospects for promotion?		
What do you think of your job?		
What exactly does your work involve?		

Work in pairs. Complete the second column with details about your partner's job. Then write a description of your partner's job.

Discovering the Sights ✂ for use with Section A3, Unit 1

Look through the information about Edinburgh below and on the next page *as quickly as possible* to find the following places. Write down the number of each place.

1. the most picturesque of the historic buildings in Edinburgh
2. a little Norman chapel built by Queen Margaret in 1076
3. 3,000,000 books
4. the home of the Scottish parliament from 1639 to 1707
5. the official residence of the Queen when she is in Scotland
6. the biggest colony of penguins in captivity
7. the building erected in 1591 and now a museum
8. the High Kirk of Edinburgh
9. the largest artifical ski slope in Britain
10. the best known monument in Edinburgh

EDINBURGH

1 THE CASTLE. This ancient fortress overlooking the gardens of Princes Street is full of historic interest. Rebuilt in the 7th century by Edwin, King of Northumbria, it has a beautiful little Norman Chapel built by the saintly Queen Margaret in 1076. This is Edinburgh's oldest building still in use. The Royal apartments, the Great Banqueting Hall, the Scottish Crown, Sceptre and Sword of State are among other items of interest. The Castle also contains one of the most beautiful War Memorials in the world.

2 ST GILES' CATHEDRAL. The Cathedral, the High Kirk of Edinburgh, is the very heart of Scotland and survivor of churches that existed on the site before history was written. It is an imposing and lofty Gothic building with many historic memorials and monuments.

3 PARLIAMENT HOUSE. Behind St Giles' Cathedral. The Scots Parliament met here from 1639 until the Union of Scotland and England in 1707. It is now the home of Scotland's supreme courts, both civil and criminal. The great south window depicts the inauguration of the Court of Session by King James V in 1532.

4 JOHN KNOX'S HOUSE. The most picturesque of the historic dwellings of Edinburgh. Built in 1490, the house is reputed to have been the manse of John Knox, when he was minister of St Giles'. The timber gallery and hand painted ceiling are unusual features, and there are some noteworthy items connected with the great Reformer.

5 PALACE OF HOLYROODHOUSE. The Palace is the official residence of Her Majesty the Queen when she is in Edinburgh. It originated as a guest house for the Abbey of Holyrood, now a ruin adjoining the Palace. When King James IV made Edinburgh the Capital of Scotland at the beginning of the 16th century the guest house became a Royal Palace. The Palace as seen today is mainly the work of King Charles II who began rebuilding in 1671. Mary Queen of Scots is the most famous historical figure associated with the Palace.

6 SCOTT MONUMENT. The Scott Monument, in East Princes Street Gardens, is the most conspicuous and best known monument in Edinburgh. Completed in 1844 to the design of George Meikle Kemp, the monument is in the form of a Gothic spire 200 feet high with a statue of Sir Walter Scott, by Sir John Steell, installed under the canopy of the arches, in 1846. The climb up the 287 steps to the top of the tower is well worthwhile for the magnificent views of the city.

7 NATIONAL GALLERY OF SCOTLAND. Opened in 1859 the National Gallery of Scotland, at the foot of the Mound, Princes Street, is one of the more important of the smaller galleries of Europe.

8 ROYAL SCOTTISH ACADEMY. The Royal Scottish Academy of Painting, Sculpture and Architecture, at the Mound, Princes Street, was founded in 1826 to promote the fine arts in Scotland. The annual exhibition is held from late April until early August. It reopens later in August for the special Festival Exhibition.

9 SCOTTISH NATIONAL GALLERY OF MODERN ART. Opened in 1960, this gallery in Inverleith House, Royal Botanic Garden, contains European, English and Scottish paintings, graphic art and sculpture of the 20th century.

10 CITY OF EDINBURGH ART CENTRE. The Art Centre, in the historic Hamilton building, at Regent Road, houses the City's Permanent Collection of Painting and Sculpture. This covers Scottish painting over the last 100 years.

11 CANONGATE TOLBOOTH. Situated in the Canongate part of the Royal Mile, this building is an interesting survival of municipal architecture in the 16th century. It was built in 1591. It is now a city museum containing, among other items, the J. Telfer Dunbar collection of Highland dress.

12 CANONGATE CHURCH. Farther down, on the same side as the Tolbooth, is Canongate Church, built as the parish church of the burgh of Canongate in 1688.

13 HUNTLY HOUSE. Opposite the Tolbooth is Huntly House, a reconstructed town dwelling of 1517, now the principal museum of local history. It contains many items of historic interest.

14 ACHESON HOUSE. Near Huntly House, on the same side of the street, is an interesting old house built in 1633. It is now the headquarters of the Scottish Craft Centre.

15 MUSEUM OF CHILDHOOD. This unique museum is situated in Hyndford's Close, High Street, almost opposite John Knox's House. It has an extremely large collection of historical toys, books, costumes, dolls, pictures and other items relating to childhood in the past.

16 LADY STAIR'S HOUSE. Lady Stair's House, in the Lawnmarket section of the Royal Mile, was built in 1622. It now belongs to the City of Edinburgh and contains important collections of manuscripts and relics of three famous figures in Scottish literature. Robert Burns, Sir Walter Scott and R. L. Stevenson.

17 GLADSTONE'S LAND. Adjoining James' Close and fronting Lawnmarket, is a tall, handsome building called Gladstone's Land. This dignified 17th-century house is a fine example of the period. Owned by the National Trust for Scotland, it is the headquarters of the Saltire Society.

continued

18 CITY CHAMBERS. Opposite St Giles' are the City Chambers, where the Lord Provost, Magistrates and Members of the Town Council of the City of Edinburgh meet.

19 GREYFRIARS KIRK. The Kirk of the Greyfriars, situated in Forrest Road, at the southern end of George IV Bridge, is famous as the scene of the signing of the National Covenant in 1638. The graveyard is worth visiting for its range of stately monuments and ornate tombstones commemorating famous citizens of old Edinburgh. The statue of Greyfriars' Bobby is outside the gate, at Candlemaker Row.

20 NATIONAL LIBRARY OF SCOTLAND. The library in George IV Bridge, founded in 1682 by the Faculty of Advocates, has enjoyed the privilege of copyright deposit since 1710. With nearly 3,000,000 books and an extensive collection of manuscripts it is one of the four largest libraries in Great Britain.

21 ROYAL SCOTTISH MUSEUM. This museum, in Chambers Street, houses the national collections of decorative arts of the world archaeology, ethnography, natural history, geology, technology and science. Its displays range from primitive art to space material, from ceramics to fossils, from birds to working models in the Hall of Power.

22 SCOTTISH NATIONAL PORTRAIT GALLERY. Founded in 1882 to 'illustrate Scottish history by likenesses of the chief actors in it', it contains a fascinating collection of portraits of famous Scots, covering a period from the mid-sixteenth century to the present day.

23 NATIONAL MUSEUM OF ANTIQUITIES. Situated in the same building as the Scottish National Portrait Gallery. In Queen Street, this interesting museum contains the most representative collection of the history and everyday life of Scotland from the Stone Age to modern times.

24 ROYAL COMMONWEALTH POOL. This magnificent pool at Dalkeith Road, built to international standards in 1970, has accommodation for 1,100 bathers and 2,000 spectators and large social areas. There are facilities also for high divers and toddlers.

25 PORTOBELLO OPEN AIR POOL. The large open-air bathing pool at Portobello is a Mecca for swimmers in the summer months. It has accommodation for 3,000 swimmers and 6,000 spectators and a wave-making machine.

26 HILLEND SKI CENTRE. Hillend Ski Centre on the Pentland Hills is the largest artificial ski-slope in Britain, it offers facilities for skiers throughout the year. There is a chair lift and walkers and sightseers enjoy a magnificent view of the surrounding countryside from the Pentland peaks.

27 MEADOWBANK SPORTS CENTRE. Meadowbank Sports Centre is a complex with facilities for upwards of thirty sports and is situated within easy reach of the city centre. It consists of a main outdoor arena with a 400 metres 'Tartan' athletics track and a seating capacity of 15,000. The indoor centre has three large multi-purpose sports halls with spectator accommodation for up to 2,300.

28 ROYAL BOTANIC GARDEN. The Royal Botanic Garden, at Inverleith Row – car parking Arboretum Road – has a world-famous rock garden, unique exhibition plant houses showing a great range of exotic plants displayed as indoor landscapes and a plant exhibition hall displaying many aspects of botany and horticulture.

29 LAURISTON CASTLE. This is a country mansion of great charm, situated at Davidson's Mains, about five miles from the city centre. It has a turreted and corbelled 16th-century tower. Situated in beautiful grounds overlooking the Firth of Forth, the house is now a City museum containing fine furniture, Flemish tapestries, "Blue John" ware, etc.

30 THE ZOO. The Scottish national Zoological Park is 75 acres of open enclosures and animal houses. It is world famous for its penguins (the largest colony of Antarctic penguins in captivity) and its collection of mammals, birds, reptiles, fish and anthropods contains all the favourites generally found in the most up-to-date zoos. It is a must for all visitors with children.

Places in Britain for use with Section D2, Unit 1

Card 1
York: First a Roman settlement, then the northern capital of the Normans, the walled city of York has been prosperous since its wool-trading days. Its cathedral, known as The Minister, took two and a half centuries to complete and is famous for its mediaeval stained-glass windows. York is in the North-East of England, north-west of Hull, north-east of the Peak District.

Card 2
The Norfolk Broads: The Broads, not far from Great Yarmouth on the eastern coast of England, are open stretches of water, streams and man-made canals, all linked together in 200 miles of navigable waterways. It is now a popular centre for sailing, cruising and boating holidays and has a varied bird life and many fine windmills.

Card 3
Stonehenge: This mysterious group of standing stones, situated in the middle of the chalk plains of Salisbury in southern England, date from 1800 BC. Modern druids, or sun worshippers, still carry out an ancient ritual here on midsummer's day, June 21st, when the sun rises exactly over the Heelstone.

Card 4
The Giant's Causeway: This impressive rock formation is situated on the coast not far from Portrush in Northern Ireland. It was caused by unusual cooling of volcanic lava many thousands of years ago, which formed into huge polygonal columns. Invading armies have been known to fire on the section known as 'the chimney tops' believing them to be the chimneys of a castle.

Card 5
The Lake District: This beautiful region in the North-West of England was the inspiration for Wordsworth and other English Romantic poets. It is a region of lakes, that fill the valleys gouged out by Ice Age glaciers, waterfalls, rolling fells (hills) and inviting mountains.

Card 6
Belfast: The capital of Northern Ireland was an insignificant village until the arrival of French Hugenot refugees in the 17th century who developed its linen industry. More recently, when the sand-blocked river mouth was cleared, the city became an important shipbuilding centre.

Card 7
Loch Ness: This 24-mile long loch (lake) near Inverness in Scotland is said to be inhabited by a monster, Nessie. Sightings have estimated her length as anything from 25 ft. to 70 ft, and she could belong to the fish, reptile or invertebrate family. It is difficult to be more precise as she only puts in unpredictable and brief appearances!

Card 8
Snowdon: Snowdon, at 3560 feet, is the highest peak of the dramatic mountainous area of North-West Wales, south of Bangor. It can be climbed on foot but there is also a rack-and-pinion railway that winds up steep gradients to the summit. It is the second highest mountain in Britain, after Ben Nevis in Scotland.

Card 9
Ben Nevis: Britain's highest mountain at 4406 feet, Ben Nevis is a granite mass more than 500 million years old. From Fort William, lying to the west, there is a narrow stony, five mile path to the peak. The northerly route is a tough climb and can be attempted only by very experienced mountaineers.

Card 10
Edinburgh: East of Glasgow, on the Firth of Forth, is the beautiful capital city of Scotland, Edinburgh, dominated by its imposing castle complex. The Royal Palace, in which Mary Queen of Scots gave birth to James VI, houses the Scottish Crown Jewels, which are older than those in the Tower of London.

Card 11
Cardiff: Cardiff, the capital of Wales, is situated on the south coast in the Bristol Channel. It changed from a small town to a prosperous city during the Industrial Revolution in the late 19th century, when its port became important in the growing Welsh coal trade. A beautiful city of parks, delightful buildings, and a castle dating from Roman times, Cardiff is also world-famous for its home of Welsh rugby; Cardiff Arms Park.

Card 12
Exmoor: In the South-West of England, Devon and Somerset boast the romantic moorland of Exmoor associated with R.D. Blackmore's *Lorna Doone*. Less wild than Dartmoor to the south, it is heather and secret valleys, wild ponies, buzzards and red deer, lonely farmhouses, undecorated dark horizons, and views, on a clear day, across the Bristol Channel to Wales.

Card 13
The Cotswolds: on the West Midlands the Cotswold hills lie on a south-west north-east line, starting just north of Bristol and ending south of Stratford. Great flocks of sheep have grazed these hills since Roman times, and the local yellowish limestone in which the charming villages are built, gives a pleasing uniformity to this pretty rural area.

Card 14
Aberdeen: The busy port and University City of Aberdeen in North-East Scotland is an important centre for the comparatively new North Sea Oil industry. This granite city is surrounded by a region of heathery moorland, wooded valleys, and many many castles, including Balmoral, the favorite summer residence of the Royal Family.

Card 15
Peak District: A National Park; the unspoilt Peak District of Derbyshire lies at the southern end of The Penines – the backbone of England. A popular venue for ramblers, the area is also a geologists' delight as it contains the only mines for the semi-precious Blue John in the world. In the heart of the area is Buxton, the picturesque Victorian Spa town.

Becoming a Picture for use with Section A3, Unit 2

Role cards ✂ for use with Section D4, Unit 2

Card A		Card B		Card C	
You'd like to . . .	**You wouldn't like to . . .**	**You'd like to . . .**	**You wouldn't like to . . .**	**You'd like to . . .**	**You wouldn't like to . . .**
play golf	go fishing	go out for a meal	play golf	have a sauna	play golf
visit an art gallery	go sightseeing	go fishing	go sightseeing	go sightseeing	go fishing
go to the cinema	go to a museum	go to the cinema	visit an art gallery	go out for a meal	visit an art gallery
have a sauna	go for a walk	go to a museum	go for a walk	go on a coach trip	go to a museum
	go out for a meal	go on a coach trip	have a sauna	go for a walk	go to the cinema

Talking Points ✂ for use with Section B2, Unit 3

What is the difference between these sentences?
I've ridden a camel! I rode a camel in Egypt two years ago and it was very uncomfortable!

Work in pairs. Ask your partner about the things he/she has done and complete the chart. Ask about things which interest you!

Have your ever . . .	When . . . ?	Where . . . ?	What . . . like?
. . . a Shakespeare play?			
. . . London?			
. . . .			
. . . .			
. . . .			
. . . .			
. . . .			
. . . .			
What interesting things have you done in your lifetime?			
. . . .			
. . . .			
. . . .			
. . . .			
. . . .			
. . . .			

Now tell the class about your partner.

Rings and Things for use with Section B2, Unit 4

A Rings and Things
Your partner has got some rings which are different from yours and some which are the same. Describe your rings and find the matching pairs.

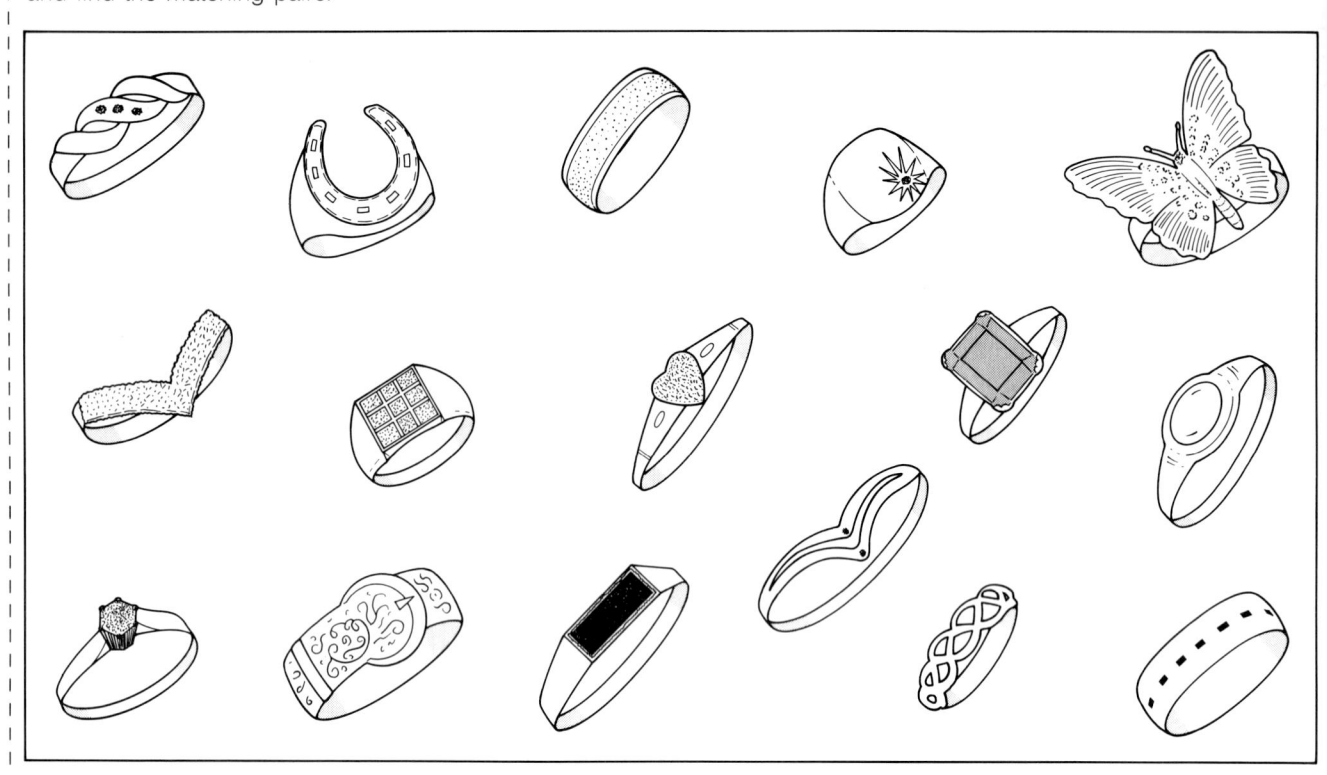

B Rings and Things
Your partner has got some rings which are the same as yours and some which are different. Find the ones which are different.

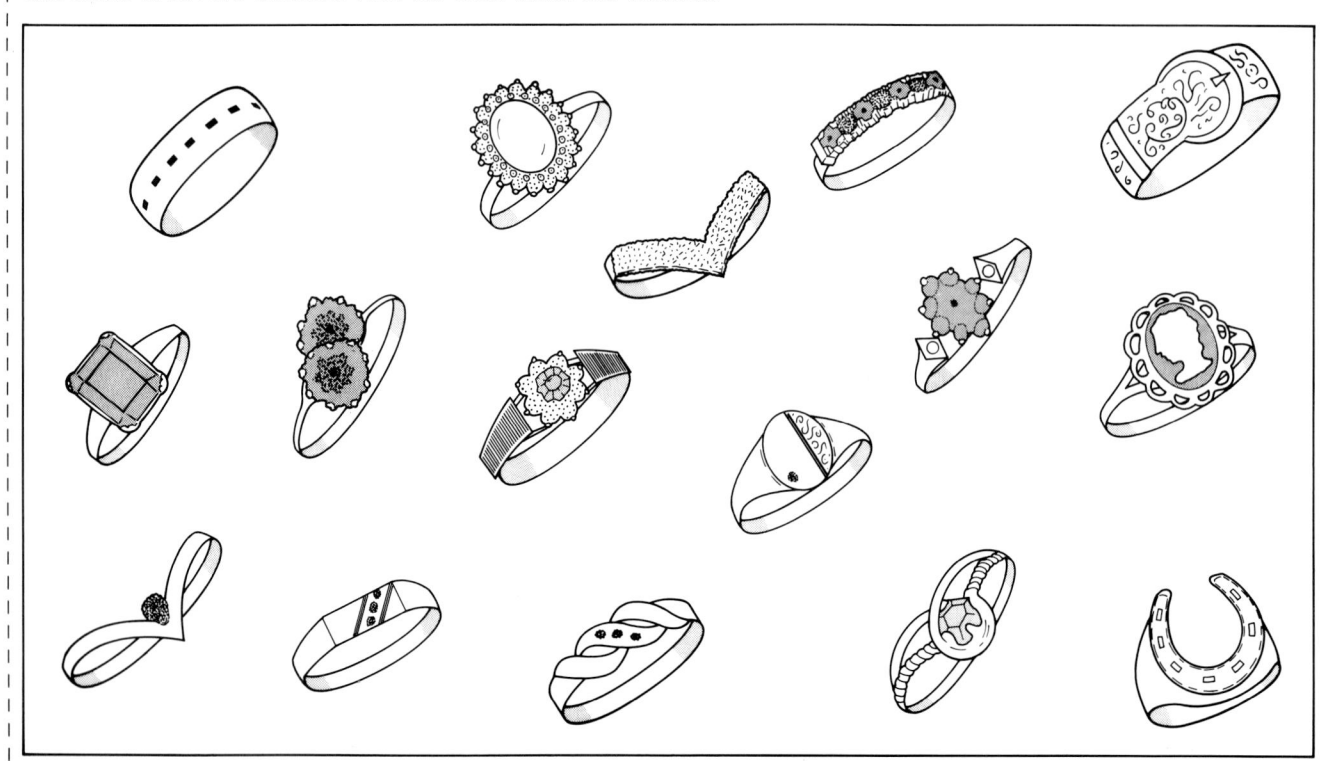

Creative Fruit ✂ for use with Section C, Unit 4

In pairs make notes of your ideas as you follow the steps below. Use the language chart to help you.

Step 1
LOOK at the fruit or vegetable. Describe it in as much detail as you can. Describe it as if you were a giant/a dwarf/a martian.

Step 2
SMELL the fruit or vegetable and follow the same instructions.

Step 3
FEEL the fruit or vegetable (eyes closed perhaps) and follow the same instructions.

Now cut open the fruit or vegetable and repeat steps 1, 2 and 3.

Step 4
TASTE the fruit or vegetable and try to find the words to describe it.

Step 5
Using your notes, write a short poem about your fruit. Remember, modern poetry needn't rhyme!

It	looks	(+ adj.)
	smells	fresh
	feels	soft
	tastes	delicious etc.

It looks (etc.) like a	(+ noun)
	ball
	bomb etc.

It looks as	if	(+ phrase)
	though	it has been painted.
		it is difficult to eat.

Dream a little! 'If I was a giant it would look . . .'

Who Are You ✂ for use with Section E2, Unit 4

RED PERSON
Identifies with the physical body. Finds security in health, fitness, strength and sexual prowess. Likes food, and exciting pursuits. Lives in a time world that is immediate. Easily gets bored sitting around. Needs to be on the move.
Positive aspects: Sportsman/woman. Works hard, plays hard.
Negative aspects: Lethargic, therefore may get fat. Prefers eating to exercising. Physical bully.

GREEN PERSON
Identifies with own ego. Self-possessed and highly motivated. Very often in business but also project leaders in all walks of life. Need to be recognised as apart from the herd. Easily hurt if ignored. Love – expressed passionately.
Positive aspects: Using personal power and money to help others. Deep emotional caring. Selfless behaviour.
Negative aspects: Seeking power over others. Manipulative. Uses emotional blackmail. Highly possessive.

VIOLET PERSON
Identifies with creative imagination. See themselves as problem-solvers. Inventors, artists, musicians, and those that give society a new image to live by, e.g. Jesus, Hitler, Napoleon, Buddha.
Positive aspects: Clear creativity that inspires others to heights of mental and emotional exhileration.
Negative aspects: Inspiring others to fulfil projects that expand their own ego image. Very often this is done through fear, e.g. S.S., Inquisition.

INDIGO PERSON
Identifies with the very centre of being. meditative and intuitive. Feels one with nature and the entire cosmos. Enjoy their own company, beauty and harmony. Pacifist. Love – expressed through warm soft caring which is often non-verbal and non-sexual.
Positive aspects: Creator of harmonious environments and atmospheres. Healing presence. Deep and immediate understanding of another inner world.
Negative aspects: Aloof and distant. Cannot relate to the rest of society. Very often living in isolation. Nervous and scared of other people, especially red and green.

ORANGE PERSON
Identifies with friends, family and groups. Finds security in friendship and companionship. Needs to feel that they are accepted and not challenged. Followers of fashion and social trends. Love – the orange person is sensual and needs lots of cuddles.
Positive aspects: Community workers, voluntary workers. Party-going and fun-loving. Very tactile. Supportive of others.
Negative aspects: Gossip. Back-biting and prejudiced. Identifying people outside the group as 'them' and not 'us', and ignoring them.

Alibi ✂ for use with Section B2, Unit 6

Group A
Last night a bank was robbed between 8 o'clock and 10 o'clock and the police suspect you might be involved. You weren't. However, you were in the casino gambling. You promised your wife/husband you wouldn't go to the casino again as you frequently spend a lot of money. You did so last night. You are afraid to tell the police the truth as you are sure your wife/husband will find out about it. How are you going to answer the policeman's questions?

Group B
You are policemen. There was a robbery last night between 8 o'clock and 10 o'clock. You have to interview student A, as he/she was seen near the scene of the crime at about nine o'clock. You want to know where he/she was going and if he/she has any witnesses. He/she is only one of several people being interviewed by the police.

Everyone in Group A find a partner in Group B. Carry out the interview.

List of voluntary help agencies/charities in the UK — for use with Section A3, Unit 7

The Colostomy Welfare Group
38/9 Eccleston Square (2nd Floor), London SW1V 1PB (01-828 5175)

Cruse, The National Organization for the Widowed and their Children
Cruse House, 126 Sheen Road, Richmond, Surrey TW9 1UR (01-940 4818/9047)

The Cystic Fibrosis Research Trust
5 Blyth Road, Bromley, Kent BR1 3RS (01-464 7211)

The Disabled Living Foundation
346 Kensington High Street, London W14 8NS (01-602 2491)

Dr Barnardo's
Tanners Lane, Barkingside, Ilford, Essex LG6 1QG (01-550 8822)

The Family Planning Association
Margaret Pyke House, 27 Mortimer Street, London W1A 4QW (01-636 7866)

Gingerbread
35 Wellington Street, London WC2E 7BN (01-240 0953)

The Ileostomy Association of Great Britain and Ireland
1st Floor, 23 Winchester Road, Basingstoke, Hampshire RG21 1UE (Basingstoke 21288)

The Marie Curie Memorial Foundation
124 Sloane Street, London SW1X 9BP (01-730 9157)

The Mastectomy Association of Great Britain
1 Colworth Road, Croydon CR0 7AD (01-654 8643)

The Migraine Trust
45 Great Ormond Street, London WC1N 3HD (01-278 2676)

The Multiple Sclerosis Society of Great Britain and Northern Ireland
286 Munster Road, London SW6 6BE (01-381 4022)

The Muscular Dystrophy Group of Great Britain
Natrass House, 35 Macauley Road, Clapham SW4 0QP (01-720 8055)

The National Society for Cancer Relief
Michael Sobell House, 30 Dorset Square, London NW1 6QL (01-402 8125)

The Nursing and Hospital Careers Information Centre
121 Edgware Road, London W2 2HX

The Psoriasis Association
7 Milton Street, Northampton NN2 7JG (Northampton 711129)

The Royal Association for Disability and Rehabilitation (RADAR)
25 Mortimer Street, London W1N 8AB (01-637 5400)

The Royal National Institute for the Blind
224 Great Portland Street, London W1N 6AA (01-388 1266)

The Royal National Institute for the Deaf
105 Gower Street, London WC1E 6AH (01-387 8033)

Royal Society for the Prevention of Accidents
Cannon House, The Priory, Queensway, Birmingham B4 6BS

St Andrew's Ambulance Association
36 Palmerston Place, Edinburgh 12 (031-225 1511)

St John Ambulance Brigade
1 Grosvenor Crescent, London SW1X 7EF (01-235 5231)

The Samaritans
Headquarters: 17 Uxbridge Road, Slough SL1 1SN (Slough 32713/4)
For local Samaritans, see telephone directory

The Spastics Society
12 Park Crescent, London W1N 4EQ (01-636 5020)

The Spinal Injuries Association
126 Albert Street, London NW1 7NF (01-267 6111)

Age Concern England (National Old People's Welfare Council)
Bernard Sunley House, 60 Pitcairn Road, Mitcham, Surrey CR4 3LL (01-640 5431)

Alcoholics Anonymous
P.O. Box 514, 11 Redcliffe Gardens, London SW10 9BG (01-352 5493/9779)

The Arthritis and Rheumatism Council for Research in Great Britain and the Commonwealth
8/10 Charing Cross Road, London WC2H 0HN (01-240 0871)

The Association for Spina Bifida and Hydrocephalus
Tavistock House North, Tavistock Square, London WC1H 9HJ (01-388 1382)

The British Diabetic Association
3/6 Alfred Place, London WC1E 7EE (01-636 7355/8)

The British Epilepsy Society
3/6 Alfred Place, London WC1E 7ED (01-580 2704)

The British Polio Fellowship
Bell Close, West End Road, Ruislip, Middlesex HA4 6LP (Ruislip 75515)

The British Red Cross Society
9 Grosvenor Crescent, London SW1X 7EJ (01-235 5454)

The British Rheumatism and Arthritis Association
6 Grosvenor Crescent, London SW1X 7ER (01-235 0902)

The Chest, Heart and Stroke Association
Tavistock House North, Tavistock Square, London WC1H 9JE (01-387 3012/4)

Problem Advice — for use with Section B4, Unit 7

Advice cards

How about . . . ?	Why don't you . . . ?	Couldn't you . . . ?	What about . . . ?
Why not . . . ?	You should . . .	As your mother/father, I'd suggest that you . . .	If I were you, I'd . . .
You'd better (not) . . .	How about . . . ?	Why don't you . . . ?	Couldn't you . . . ?
What about . . . ?	Why not . . . ?	You ought to . . .	As your doctor, I'd advise you to . . .
If I were you, I'd . . .	You'd better . . .		

Problem cards

I'm very depressed.	My landlady is very rude to me.	I don't know what to do when I return to my own country.	I'm in love with someone 15 years older than me.
I can't cook.	I need to drive but I'm very nervous.	I want to get a job in England.	I want to buy a present for my father – any ideas?
I'm too fat.	I've got a terrible headache.	My boy/girl friend is going around with another girl/boy. What do you suggest?	My hair always looks horrible.
I keep forgetting things.	I can't speak English very well.	What kind of car do you think I should buy?	I want some new clothes – where should I buy them?

Roleplay ✂ for use with Section B4, Unit 7

Father
You are worried about your son. You think he should be doing more at school – his reports have not been good. You blame a good deal of this on his mother who is altogether too possessive. You would like to see him more involved in sport.

Daughter
You think that your parents moan too much about your brother. You think he is basically a good boy but involved with a bad crowd. You do, however, feel that he could do more work at school.

Mother
You love your son but you believe he has become too involved with a gang of bad lads. They influence his behaviour – punk haircut, bad language, etc. He drinks and smokes too much for your liking.

Son
You are fed up with your parents criticizing you all the time. You want to be free to do what you want. You have some good mates and enjoy going out with them. You don't like school much; it's boring, although you do like art.

Agreement Cards ✂ for use with Section B3, Unit 8

Smoking should be made illegal.	All women should be compelled to have their babies in hospital.	There can never be another major war.	Civil servants have no useful purpose except for using up a lot of paper.
Cars should be banned from large cities.	Intelligent life definitely exists on other planets.	Plants can talk.	Cyclists are a menace on the public highway.
Life is what you make it.	Nobody should have to live in high-rise blocks of flats.	Muggers should be shot.	There is nothing after death.
The army makes men out of boys.	All eggs should be free-range.	People who live in cities are crazy.	Space exploration is a waste of everyone's money.
It's dangerous to have animals in the home. Pets should be banned.	There is no such thing as a fair trial.	It's impossible to have everything you want.	The best things in life are free.

continued

Men who have beards are devious.	There is no such thing as ghosts.	People are too selfish these days.	Everyone is equally intelligent.
We have all had past existences.	Everybody needs someone to love.	Bringing up children is easy.	These days nobody should go hungry.

The Trouble With The World Today ✂ for use with Section D, Unit 8

A *Mr. Johnson*

You are a farmer.

Ask people if:
1 They think blood sports should be banned.
2 They think eating meat is morally wrong.

You think that fox-hunting is necessary as foxes are very bad for your farm and it's good sport. You also believe in eating meat as meat is one of the best ways to eat protein which human beings need. Also many vegetarians drink milk – they don't seem to understand that they can only have milk if calves are bred and killed because then the cow produces a lot of milk.

In your opinion:
Women should stay at home and look after the family and should not fight for social change. Marriage is one of the most important institutions in our society, necessary for the future, and women should work for peace and happiness at home: men should be the ones who work and who defend the country.

You feel that modern morals are terrible. There are too many disgusting books and films now which young children can see. There is too little censorship to protect children from the evil things in the world.

You think that most people were very happy at school, but you aren't sure that they are the 'happiest days of your life', you hated school. Some children need to stay at home and work with their parents and not to go to school, especially if they cannot do mathematics and other schoolwork. You can remember how difficult school can be if you aren't clever!

B *Miss Pringle*

You are a magazine editor.

Ask people if:
1 Women should do military service as well as men.
2 Marriage is out-dated.

You think that women are equal to men in every way. If women want to have equal rights in life then they should also take part in the defence of the country and be as active in the military as men. In your opinion there would be few wars if women had control in the military services. Women should get up and fight.

You also feel that marriage is a way of keeping women quiet and that in modern times there are other ways of looking after children than having women sitting at home and working like servants for no money. There should be nurseries for working women and women should choose if they want children but not necessarily become legally tied to one man.

In your opinion:
Blood sports are wrong. You saw a bullfight and it made you feel sick. You feel sorry for the animals as they don't know what is happening. How can such sport be a pleasure for anyone? Schooldays are certainly NOT the happiest days of your life. You have no freedom and no choice in what you do there. You learn things which are totally useless in later life and some children who are not very clever feel that they cannot ever do anything because they fail examinations. What is education really for?

You are not a vegetarian but you don't like eating meat, you feel it is wrong but isn't it also wrong to eat plants? They have feelings, too! You aren't really sure how you feel about this question. There shouldn't be censorship but you can see that it is sometimes necessary to protect children.

C *Mrs James*

You are a teacher.

Ask people if:
Schooldays are the happiest days of your life.

You feel that schooldays should be the happiest days of your life. This is the only time when you are free to learn and to enjoy yourself, and there is always something which a child can be good at. It is a time of self-discovery and of play. You had a marvellous time at school and you love teaching now.

In your opinion:
Eating meat is morally wrong. Animals have souls and we should protect all living things and not kill them. There is too much killing for no useful reasons. Also, you are a vegetarian because you feel that eating meat is not necessary for a healthy diet. There are a lot of people who haven't got enough food in the world. If there were no animals on farms, we could produce enough food to feed everyone in the world.

You also strongly disagree with blood sports. You think that hunting is terrible and shows that men are worse than animals. Animals hunt to live; men hunt for pleasure.

You don't think that marriage is out-dated. You think it is simply changing. Children need a mother and a father to be happy and secure, but women also need the freedom to go to work if they want to. Marriage these days means sharing the household jobs and sharing in the difficulties of bringing up children.

You agree with censorship but think that children can be protected too much. That is, that they should understand some of the bad side of life when they are ready to. Some people want to censor too many things which are simply part of life.

D *Mr Williams*

You are a vicar. In fact, you are '*Reverend* Williams'

Ask people if:
Censorship is necessary.

You feel that there is too little censorship in these permissive times and that people see things which are best forgotten. Children haven't got any guide lines as to what is right and what is wrong and so there is more violence. You want more censorship of television programmes and books.

In your opinion:
All animals are God's creatures and we should be kind to them and not hunt them or kill them unless we need to eat. So, you are against blood sports. However, you think that eating meat is necessary for human beings to live.

You believe that marriage is the basis of society. It is certainly not out-dated although it has changed. Men and women need each other and children need both parents to lead a happy life. Schooldays are very happy days for children. They are days of innocence and enjoyment, of learning and of growing up. Most people look back on these days with pleasure.

Women are soft and gentle creatures. God made them to preserve life and to protect life. They are not strong enough to fight and you think that they should NOT do military service as this is against everything that 'womanhood' stands for: love, children, the home, marriage, peace. However, perhaps some young women could do nursing or office work in the services.

Animal Noises for use with Section A3, Unit 9

1 Think of the characteristics of these animals and birds, and write down the 'noises' they make. There is more than one 'noise' for some of them. Choose from:

yelp roar chatter whimper hiss chirp twitter yap bellow hoot bark cackle squeal purr

a dog _____
b lion _____
c owl _____
d cat _____
e bull _____
f pig _____
g monkey _____
h bird _____
i snake _____
j hen _____

2 Many of these words can be used to express human emotions. Tick the appropriate boxes in this chart.

	with laughter	in anger	in derision	with pain	with delight	in disgust
roar						
snort						
cackle						
hoot						
squeal						
whimper						
bellow						
yelp						
purr						

3 Now fill the spaces with these words, using an appropriate tense.

chatter hiss chirp yap bark

a 'Up to your rooms immediately,' he _____
b They _____ for the whole evening, catching up on each other's news.
c 'You nasty child,' she _____ malevolently.
d 'I know! Never mind the rain! Let's go to a museum!' my aunt _____ cheerfully.
e '_____ that's all you ever do! Why can't you listen to me for a change?'

4 Which creatures were the speakers thinking of when they said these sentences? And which sentence means 'He's in a bad mood'?

a He has the hump today.
b We were stung by his remarks.
c He's always crowing about his success.
d Why are you galloping along the corridor?
e The lecturer's voice droned on and on.

Newspaper Reporter for use with Section C3, Unit 9

CIGARETTE PRICES DOWN

TELEPORT – THE NEW WAY TO TRAVEL

COLONY ON THE MOON

OIL RUNS OUT

KING KONG LOOSE

ROLLS ROYCE OUT OF BUSINESS

FREE WHISKY IN SCOTLAND

MAN WINS ELEPHANT

DROUGHT IN SWITZERLAND

RUSSIA JOINS EEC

MOTHER OF FOUR BREAKS WORLD RECORD

EX-FOOTBALLER BECOMES PRESIDENT

PIPE SMOKERS LIVE LONGER – HEALTH REPORT

CHILD LIFTS LORRY TO REACH TOY

ALIEN ROCKET LANDS IN USA

CARS BANNED IN BRITAIN

GRANNIES MUG TEENAGERS

SNOW IN SAHARA

TAXES CUT

CIVIL SERVANTS IN RIOT

FAIRIES AT THE BOTTOM OF THE GARDEN

MAN 800 YEARS OLD FOUND IN MOUNTAINS

APE MAN LIVING IN AMAZON JUNGLE

DOGS ROB BANK – STEAL £3 MILLION

Three people — for use with Section D3, Unit 9

Read the descriptions of these three people.

James is a tentative sort of person. He is unsure of himself, and very modest.

Sue is completely 'over the top'. She tends to exaggerate, and uses extravagant language.

David is very formal and old-fashioned. Where one word will do, he will use ten.

Which of the three people said these things?

1 You really can't imagine! It was the most awful sight! All that blood and gore! I was totally shattered by it! My nerves were in shreds for weeks.

2 It isn't a bad little place, is it? It seems to be about right for me and there's a sweet little garden. The view's quite nice, too; the mountains are rather pretty in the summer. I'm quite lucky, really.

3 I am aroused by the obligation to offer you my heartfelt congratulations on the successful completion of your task.

4 I confess that the odious nature of your utterance arouses my ire.

5 This is the most incredible moment of my life. I've been dying to meet you for ages, and now here you are! I'm completely overwhelmed!

6 I extend the deepest and most humble of apologies for my tardiness in utilizing the telephonic apparatus to transmit my communication.

7 How absolutely thrilling! I simply adore Rome! It's such a magnificent city! I can't wait to get there! You're an angel for inviting me!

8 I thought it was rather enjoyable, and it was quite funny in parts, now that I come to think of it. Yes, it's probably worth seeing if you like that sort of thing.

9 Hmm, it seems rather cute, quite a neat little idea, really, and simple too, with those bits of wood tied together like that. One can't help but wonder, though, if it's quite safe. It looks a little small to cross the Atlantic in. I think I might give it a miss this time round.

Feelings ✂ for use with Section D3, Unit 9

Student A

1 LONGING
You are going to retire soon. You want to retire to the country with B. You are looking forward to the fresh air, peace, good food, relaxation, gardening, and country walks. You are sure you'll find a perfect country cottage. Talk to B.

I'm longing to . . .
I'm dying to . . .
I'm happy to . . .
I'm crazy about . . .ing
It'll be marvellous to . . .
We'll be able to . . .

2 EXCITEMENT
You are 17. You are excited because you're going on holiday alone for the first time. You're going to hitch-hike with your friend and you're going to stay in Rome for a month. You can't wait to speak Italian (you learned it at school); eat Pizza; see the Colosseum and sit in the sun. You'll be able to see so many wonderful sights . . .

It'll be great/fantastic to . . .
I can't wait to . . .
I'm looking forward to . . .ing
I'm thrilled at the idea of . . .ing
Just think . . . I'll be able to . . .
At last I'll have a chance to . . .
I'm sure I'll have a lovely time . . .ing the . . .

3 DISAPPROVAL
Your daughter Juliet seems to be very obsessed with a rather nasty type of boy. You are worried about her and totally disapprove of him. You want to stop her seeing him and make her see sense. He's too old for her, he wears awful leather clothes and has long hair. His motorbike is noisy and dangerous. He's rude and what's more has no money, or prospects. He's a singer in a terrible rock and roll band. All those drugs! He isn't a handsome youth, either. Warn your daughter. There's a nice boy next door . . .

I don't like the look of . . .
I totally disapprove of . . .
I hate the way he . . .
I can't stand the way they . . .
They're all alike, they only want . . .
Can't you see that . . . ?
Surely you don't like . . . !
You can't possibly . . .
Why don't you . . . ?

4 ANGER
You've got an important exam tomorrow and you are in the library studying. There is a most annoying person near you. He/she keeps talking to himself/herself; he/she is continually eating (sweets, apples, chewing gum) and also seems to sniff once every five seconds! You simply can't get on with your work. Tell him/her.

I wish you wouldn't . . .
Do you have to . . . ?
Please stop . . .ing
Why do you keep on . . .ing?
If you don't . . ., I'll . . . !
Don't you think you should . . . ?
For goodness sake . . . !

5 DELIGHT
You've been unemployed for a year and you've just got a marvellous job. You prepared for the interview – you wore your best clothes, and practised answering questions with your friends. Also you went to bed really early. You are pleased that you studied so hard at college, too. You're sure that's why you got it. You're in the pub with another candidate.

Thank goodness I . . .
I'm so pleased that I . . .
I'm delighted that I . . .
Now I can . . .
It's lucky I . . .
Just think, now I'll be able to . . .
I really want to . . .
I'm sure it's because I . . .

6 INTEREST
You and your friend have found a mysterious cave. It looks very deep and dark. You think there might be treasure in it and you want to go and explore. Convince your friend to come.

Let's . . .
Come on, don't . . .
I wonder if . . .
Do you think there's any . . . ?
I wouldn't be surprised if . . .
I'm sure there's . . .

7 SURPRISE

You're reading a newspaper. You want to tell your friend the latest news . . .

    The Russians have landed on the moon.
    There's a dog which can speak French.
    A gorilla has escaped from the zoo.
    The British Parliament is on strike!
    A flying saucer has landed in Hyde Park!
    (Think of some *more* interesting news!)

Did you know that . . .?
Have you heard that . . .?
It says here that . . .!
Guess what, . . .!
You'll never believe it, but . . .!
What do you think of this? . . . What's more . . .

8 REGRET

You decided to take your old car on holiday with you, and now it's in ruins. You didn't bother to have it serviced before you left, and the brakes failed. You ran into a police car and you've got to go to court tomorrow. Also you broke your leg. The car is a write-off and you can't afford another. You're a taxi-driver, so if you lose your licence, you lose your job!

If only I had/hadn't . . .
I wish I had . . .
Why did I . . .?
What on earth made me . . .?
I must have been mad to . . .
And now I won't be able to . . .
I'll never . . .
How on earth can I . . .?

9 WORRY

Grandma is 75. She's been in hospital and now she's back in her home again. You are worried because she's so old and alone and she lives miles away. You don't think she'll be able to cook, clean, go shopping. She also smokes like a chimney and forgets where she puts her cigarettes. The house is old and damp, too, but she refuses any help.

I do hope she's . . .
I wonder if she'll be able to . . .
She'll never . . .
What if she . . .
Do you think we should . . .?
Supposing she . . .!
I think I ought to . . .

continued

Feelings — for use with Section D3, Unit 9

Student B

1 RELUCTANCE
You are going to retire soon. You aren't happy because A wants to retire to the country, and you're sure you'll be bored there. You hate gardening and walking, you prefer the busy city life. You're sure you'll feel really old when you stop working and meeting new people. You like to be active and you'll miss your local pub. The idea of a country cottage isn't that pleasing either. Tell A how you feel.

I can't stand the thought of . . .
I don't like the idea of . . .
I don't really fancy . . .ing
I'd hate to . . .
I'd much prefer to . . .
I'm quite content to . . .
I'd miss . . .ing
We won't be able to . . . if we . . .

2 APPREHENSION
Your teenage son/daughter is going off hitch-hiking to Rome with a friend. It's the first time he/she's been away alone and you're worried about what might happen. It's dangerous — all those funny people giving them lifts — they might have an accident! You won't be able to contact them and they haven't got a lot of money. Talk to him/her about your fears, and warn him/her of the dangers.

But you might . . .
Supposing . . .
What if . . .?
How will I know if . . .?
How long are you . . .?
Why don't you . . .?
I'd rather you . . .

3 ADMIRATION
You are Juliet and you're 15. You've just met the most fantastic boy. He's handsome, charming, he's tall and clever. He writes you poetry! He's got a 1,000 cc motorbike and wears a lovely leather jacket, *and* he plays lead guitar for a pop group as well as being the singer. He writes their songs. He dances beautifully and his voice . . . ! He's 19. Tell your mum/dad.

I love the way he . . .
I adore the . . .
I'm crazy about his . . .
He's so good at . . .ing
I can't help . . . when he . . .
It's the way he . . . that really drives me wild!
                     makes me . . . !

4 IRRITATION
You're working quite happily in the library when a person near you starts sighing and glaring at you. You don't understand why. You've got a lot of work to do tonight, because you've got an exam tomorrow. You're fed up, though, because you've got an awful cold and it's probably because the flat you live in is cold. The electricity board have turned off the electricity, just to add to your problems, so you can't cook! You're starving! You're eating snacks until the library closes, then you'll go home to bed. But that stupid person is most irritating. Tell him/her.

What on earth's wrong?
Why can't you . . .?
How many times are you going to . . .?
Why don't you . . .!
For crying out loud! I can't help . . .ing!
Can't you see I . . .?
What would *you* do if you . . .?

5 DISAPPOINTMENT
You're desperate for a job. You have been unemployed for over a year and don't know how much longer you can stand living with your relatives. Trouble is that last night you felt so depressed that you went out and didn't get home until late. You felt terrible for the interview this morning. You were a bit late, you couldn't find any clean clothes and didn't have time to clean your shoes. Life can be so unfair. You worked hard at college, had all the right qualifications and still you didn't get the job. Tell A.

I can't understand why . . .
What a fool I was to . . .
I wish I'd . . .
I can't think why I . . .
They should have . . .
Why do *you* think I . . .?
I suppose I could've . . .
I don't know what to . . .

6 UNCERTAINTY
You and your friend find a dangerous-looking cave. It's very dark and you're sure there's some horrible thing living inside. You're frightened and want to continue with your walk. Tell him/her so.

There might be . . .
Hadn't we better . . .?
Don't you think it's . . .?
Come on. Let's . . .
I don't think we should.

7 INDIFFERENCE

Your friend is reading the newspaper and always insists on telling you the latest news. You really aren't interested and this time you aren't going to pretend to be. You're very busy writing a report which must be in tomorrow. That's far more important than anything in the gossipy old newspaper which your friend reads.

I couldnt care less!
So what?
Oh.
Mmm.
It's nothing to do with me.
Why should I care?
What's that to me?
Uh . . . huh . . .

8 UNSYMPATHETIC

Your friend is really stupid. He/she took an old car on holiday and insisted that it would be fine. You tried to warn him/her to have it serviced first, or at least to have the brakes tested . . . and now he/she's moaning about an accident. He/she ran into a police car of all things! And now there is to be a court case. If he/she loses his/her licence it's his/her own fault!

What did you expect then . . .?!
It's your own fault . . .
I told you to . . .
I warned you about . . .
You should/shouldn't have . . .
Don't expect any sympathy from me! Why didn't you . . .?

9 REASSURANCE

Grandma is 75 and she's been ill but she's fine now. She's a marvellous old lady, quite capable of looking after herself. She might be old but she's more lively than you are! She drinks, smokes, even swears and is the fastest driver in the village where she lives! She's got a lot of friends too and doesn't want any help from you. Tell A.

Don't worry about . . .
She's quite capable of . . .ing!
She doesn't need . . .
She can . . .
I shouldn't worry about . . .
I'm sure she'd rather . . .

The First Men — for use with Section D2, Unit 10

> 5
>
> 'And our children can't kill anybody,' I said. 'We, the adults, can do things that we know are wrong, but that's the one thing that the children can't do. They can't kill. Am I right Michael?'
> 'Yes, you're right. We must do it slowly and carefully, and the world mustn't know what we're doing. We need three years. Can you get us three years, Jean?'
> 'I'll get it,' I said.
> 'And we need all of you; we've always needed you. We love you and need you - please stay with us.'
> We got the three years, and the children made the grey, cold barrier round us. It's easy, the children tell me. As far as I can understand, they changed the <u>time</u> of the reservation, and now the world outside lives a few minutes in the future. We can see you, but you can't see us. From inside, we can go outside, into the future. I did this when we were doing experiments with the barrier. It's easy - you feel cold for a minute, that's all. And we can come back through the barrier again, but you'll understand that I can't explain that to you.
> So that's what happened, Harry. We shall never see each other again, but Mark and I are happier than we have ever been. Man will change, and there will be no death, only love and full understanding.
>
> All my love,
>
> Jean

Felton finished reading, and the two men looked at each other. Finally Eggerton said, 'We must break that barrier and try to get through it – you know that, don't you?'

'Yes,' said Felton, but his face was white.

'It will be easier now that your sister has explained it.'

'I don't think so,' Felton said. He felt very tired. 'I don't think she *has* explained it.'

'Not to you and me, perhaps. But my people will work on it. They'll find the answer. They always do.'

'Perhaps not this time.'

'Oh, yes, they will. You see, we must stop it. Those children are dangerous to society, to the world. They were right – we must kill them. It's sad, but there it is.'

True Love

A complete short story by Isaac Asimov

My name is Joe. That is what my colleague, Milton Davidson, calls me. He is a programmer and I am a computer program. I am part of the Multivac-complex and am connected with other parts all over the world. I know everything. Almost everything.

I am Milton's private program. His Joe. He understands more about programming than anyone in the world, and I am his experimental model. He has made me speak better than any other computer can.

'It is just a matter of matching sounds to symbols, Joe,' he told me. 'That's the way it works in the human brain even though we still don't know what symbols there are in the brain. I know the symbols in yours, and I can match them to words, one-to-one.' So I talk. I don't think I talk as well as I think, but Milton says I talk very well. Milton has never married, though he is nearly forty years old. He has never found the right woman, he told me. One day he said, 'I'll find her yet, Joe. I'm going to find the best. I'm going to have true love and you're going to help me. I'm tired of improving you in order to solve the problems of the world. Solve *my* problem. Find me true love.'

I said, 'What is true love?'

'Never mind. That is abstract. Just find me the ideal girl. You are connected to the Multivac-complex so you can reach the data banks of every human being in the world. We'll eliminate them all by groups and classes until we're left with only one person. The perfect person. She will be for me.'

I said, 'I am ready.'

He said, 'Eliminate all men first.'

It was easy. His words activated symbols in my molecular valves. I could reach out to make contact with the accumulated data on every human being in the world. At his words, I withdrew from 3,784,982,874 men. I kept contact with 3,786,118,000 women.

He said, 'Eliminate all younger than twenty-five, all older than forty. Then eliminate all with an IQ under 120; all with a height under 150 centimetres.'

He gave me exact measurements; he eliminated women with living children; he eliminated women with various genetic characteristics. 'I'm not sure about eye color,' he said. 'Let that go for a while. But no red hair. I don't like red hair.'

After two weeks, we were down to 235 women. They all spoke English very well. Milton said he didn't want a language problem. Even computer-translation would be in the way at intimate moments.

'I can't interview 235 women,' he said. 'It would take too much time, and people would discover what I am doing.'

'It would make trouble,' I said. Milton has arranged me to do things I wasn't designed to do. No one knew about that.

'It's none of their business,' he said, and the skin on his face grew red. 'I tell you what, Joe. I will bring in holographs, and you check the list for similarities.'

He brought in holographs of women. 'These are three beauty contest winners,' he said. 'Do any of the 235 match?'

Eight were very good matches and Milton said, 'Good, you have their data banks. Study requirements and needs in the job market and arrange to have them assigned here. One at a time, of course.' He thought a while, moved his shoulders up and down, and said. 'Alphabetical order.'

That is one of the things I am not designed to do. Shifting people from job to job for personal reasons is called manipulation. I could do it now because Milton had arranged it. I wasn't supposed to do it for anyone but him, though.

The first girl arrived a week later. Milton's face turned red when he saw her. He spoke as though it were hard to do so. They were together a great deal and he paid no attention to me. One time he said, 'Let me take you to dinner.'

The next day he said to me, 'It was no good, somehow. There was something missing. She is a beautiful woman, but I did not feel any touch of true love. Try the next one.'

It was the same with all eight. They were much alike. They smiled a great deal and had pleasant voices, but Milton always found it wasn't right. He said, 'I can't understand it, Joe. You and I have picked out the eight women who, in all the world, look the best to me. They are ideal. Why don't they please me?'

I said, 'Do you please them?'

His eyebrows moved and he pushed one fist hard against his other hand. 'That's it, Joe. It's a two-way street. If I am not their ideal, they can't act in such a way as to be my ideal. I must be their true love, too, but how do I do that?' He seemed to be thinking all that day.

The next morning he came to me and said, 'I'm going to leave it to you, Joe. All up to you. You have my data bank, and I am going to tell you everything I know about myself. You fill up my data bank in every possible detail but keep all additions to yourself.'

'What will I do with the data bank, then, Milton?'

'Then you will match it to the 235 women. No, 227. Leave out the eight you've seen. Arrange to have each undergo a psychiatric examination. Fill up their data banks and compare them with mine. Find correlations.' (Arranging psychiatric examinations is another thing that is against my original instructions.)

For weeks, Milton talked to me. He told me of his parents and his siblings. He told me of his childhood and his schooling and his adolescence. He told me of the young women he had admired from a distance. His data bank grew and he adjusted me to broaden and deepen my symbol-taking.

He said, 'You see, Joe, as you get more and more of me in you, I adjust you to match me better and better. You get to think more like me, so you understand me better. If you understand me well enough, then any woman, whose data bank is something you understand as well, would be my true love.' He kept talking to me and I came to understand him better and better.

I could make longer sentences and my expressions grew more complicated. My speech began to sound a good deal like his in vocabulary, word order and style.

I said to him one time, 'You see, Milton, it isn't a matter of fitting a girl to a physical ideal only. You need a girl who is a personal, emotional, temperamental fit to you. If that happens, looks are secondary. If we can't find the fit in these 227, we'll look elsewhere. We will find someone who won't care how you look either, or how anyone would look, if only there is the personality to fit. What are looks?'

'Absolutely,' he said. 'I would have known this if I had had more to do with women in my life. Of course, thinking about it makes it all plain now.'

We always agreed; we thought so like each other.

'We shouldn't have any trouble, now, Milton, if you'll let me ask you questions. I can see where, in your data bank, there are blank spots and unevennesses.'

What followed, Milton said, was the equivalent of a careful psychoanalysis. Of course, I was learning from the psychiatric examinations of the 227 women – on all of which I was keeping close tabs.

Milton seemed quite happy. He said, 'Talking to you, Joe, is almost like talking to another self. Our personalities have come to match perfectly.'

'So will the personality of the woman we choose.'

For I had found her and she was one of the 227 after all. Her name was Charity Jones and she was an Evaluator at the Library of History in Wichita. Her extended data bank fit ours perfectly. All the other women had fallen into discard in one respect or another as the data banks grew fuller, but with Charity there was increasing and astonishing resonance.

I didn't have to describe her to Milton. Milton had coordinated my symbolism so closely with his own I could tell the resonance directly. It fit me.

Next it was a matter of adjusting the work sheets and job requirements in such a way as to get Charity assigned to us. It must be done very delicately, so no one would know that anything illegal had taken place.

Of course, Milton himself knew, since it was he who arranged it and that had to be taken care of too. When they came to arrest him on grounds of malfeasance in office, it was, fortunately, for something that had taken place ten years ago. He had told me about it, of course, so it was easy to arrange – and he won't talk about me for that would make his offense much worse.

He's gone, and tomorrow is February 14. Valentine's Day. Charity will arrive then with her cool hands and her sweet voice. I will teach her how to operate me and how to care for me. What do looks matter when our personalities will resonate?

I will say to her, 'I am Joe, and you are my true love.'

From *The Complete Robot* by Isaac Asimov.

Who is Dave? ✂ for use with Section A2, Unit 11

Work in groups of four.
Your teacher will give each of you different information about Dave. Tell each other what you know, and work out what he does, where he lives, and what his favourite hobby is.

What does he do?	Where does he live?	What's his favourite hobby?
Teacher	Tokyo	Chess
Nurse	Paris	Football
Milkman	London	Cricket
Banker	Isfahan	Tennis
Pilot	Madrid	Skiing

Job cards

Card 1	Card 2	Card 3	Card 4
Job: He doesn't wear a uniform.	Job: He had a long training for the job.	Job: He works the same hours every day.	Job: He works with children.
Home: It's a capital city.	Home: It's abroad.	Home: The writing is not like ours.	Home: It's not far from the sea.
Hobby: It's active.	Hobby: You need a ball.	Hobby: You need more than two people.	Hobby: You usually wear white clothes.

The Black Horse Murder ✂ for use with Section B, Unit 11

The barman said that Mr Barton sometimes handed an envelope across the table to Mr Armstrong.	Mr Barton could not be found by the police after the killing.	When the man getting off the bus saw Mr Armstrong he was sitting on the car park wall holding his head.	The number thirty-eight bus stopped outside 'The Black Horse' at 10.12 p.m.
Mr Corrigan attacked Mr Armstrong at 10.10 p.m. in the car park of the 'The Black Horse' public house.	Mr Corrigan told Mr Armstrong he was going to kill him.	The barman said that Mr Armstrong and Mr Barton were regular customers in 'The Black Horse'.	The barmaid found Mr Armstrong very attractive.
It was obvious that the body had been dragged some distance.	The spanner had Mr Barton's fingerprints on it.	The barman saw Mr Barton leave the bar at 10.10 p.m.	A broken bottle with blood on it was found in 'The Black Horse' car park.
Mr Barton had been drinking on his own in 'The Black Horse'.	Mr Armstrong and Mr Barton met together from time to time in 'The Black Horse'.	The broken bottle had Mr Corrigan's fingerprints on it.	Mr Corrigan saw Mr Armstrong in the bar and started threatening him.

continued

Mr Armstrong's body was found in the back alley behind 'The Black Horse'.	Mr Corrigan and Mr Armstrong left the bar arguing at 10.05 p.m.	Mr Armstrong had been dead one hour according to a medical expert working with the police.	At 10.00 p.m. Mr Corrigan came into the bar and ordered a bottle of stout.
Mr Armstrong's body was found at 11.15 p.m.	Mr Armstrong was having an affair with Mr Corrigan's wife.	When he was discovered dead, Mr Armstrong had a large bruise and bleeding to the side of his head, and deep cuts to his throat and neck.	Mr Armstrong's blood stains were found in the car park and back alley.
A spanner with Mr Armstrong's blood on it was found in a dustbin near 'The Black Horse'.	A man getting off the number thirty-eight bus outside 'The Black Horse' saw Mr Armstrong with blood all over his face.	Mr Barton had been seen opening the boot of his car in 'The Black Horse' car park after 10.10 p.m. by a regular customer going into 'The Black Horse'.	Mr Corrigan was not at home when the police called to make enquiries after finding the body.

Tribes ✂ for use with Section D, Unit 11

Happy Tribe

You are the beautiful people. Your one aim in life is to have as many 'meaningful conversations' as possible.

One person is The Introducer. NO-ONE is allowed to talk to a member of the opposite sex until they have been officially introduced by The Introducer. Each time they wish to change partners for a new conversation they must be introduced again. The Introducer must devise a suitable ritual to perform this ceremony. If ANYONE breaks this rule they must be forcibly ejected by the other members of the tribe.

If two people feel they have had a 'meaningful conversation', they go to The Introducer who marks a *random* number against their names. If, however, they feel the conversation to have been unsatisfactory, (on the lines of only 'Lovely day, isn't it?' for example) they go on to new partners without reporting back to The Introducer.

The object of this is to have as many 'meaningful conversations' as possible. (The number written by The Introducer is not in itself important.) But you must be honest!

Trading Tribe

Your object in life is business – to make as much money as possible.

You will be given some things to trade with (for example macaroni to represent cows, beans to represent pigs and split peas to represent chickens). Your aim is to collect sets of these things by barter and exchange with other members of your tribe and then take your sets of five or ten of a kind to the BANKER who will credit your account with 100 points for a set of 10, or 10 points for a set of 5.

Method of trading: There is a strict code of practice for trading which excludes talking, (you have no time, you're too busy making money!) except for discussing other tribes when your ambassadors return.
This is the procedure: Jump, feet together, towards the person you wish to trade with. Make the noise of the animal you are collecting.
Scratch your thigh a number of times to indicate the number, (how many) you want. The other trader does the same to show what she/he wants.
If possible, make the exchange, and each trader then jumps backwards to end the transaction.
If no exchange is possible (one or both traders not having the other's requirement) jump backwards and try another trader.

To Mary ✂ for use with Section B2, Unit 12

To Mary

If I had thought you could have died,
I might have wept for thee;
But I forgot, when by your side,
That you could mortal be:
If it ever through my mind had past
That life could e'er be o'er,
And I on thee could look my last,
I would have smiled no more!

Charles Wolfe
1791–1823

Domestic Bliss ✂ for use after Section B, Unit 12

A Daughter/Son
This morning when you got up you fell over the cat who was lying at the top of the stairs waiting for someone to feed him. In order to stop yourself going head first down the stairs you grabbed the nearest thing, the landing table, and brought it crashing to the ground breaking the little ash tray your Mum/Dad had brought back from a student holiday 16 years ago. Scared of her/his reaction, you collect the bits and hide them in the nearest bin, the one in the bathroom. Your fall woke the whole household and your sister/brother emerged from her/his bedroom complaining about getting no sleep, even on a Sunday morning, and asking why no one had fed the cat. Well, that was the limit! You had a bit of an argument, a fight really, and during this your sister's/brother's face accidentally got scratched. Her/His yells of protest brought your mum/dad to the scene, to find out what was happening. She/He wouldn't listen to reason so you said something quite rude to her/him and left the house with no breakfast. Now, later in the day, you regret your behaviour, and are going to explain/apologize to your parent.

B Mother/Father
This morning you were looking forward to a Sunday morning lie-in, secretly hoping one of the children would bring you a cup of tea, when your peace was shattered by various bangings and shoutings and the children fighting. You reluctantly got up to find yourself tripping over the cat who hadn't been fed. If you've told the children once who's job it is to feed the cat, you've told them a hundred times! You stumbled into the bathroom mumbling to yourself and give a yell of pain as you tread on a piece of broken glass which you recognize as belonging to your favourite piece of sentimental memorabilia. Steaming with rage, you hop out of the bathroom in time to see your eldest child scratching her/his sister/brother. If there's one thing you will not tolerate it's bullying, so you told her/him so. She/He was very abusive and stormed out of the house. Now, later in the day, you regret having lost your temper and are going to try to make up with your child.

The Leaving of Liverpool ✂ additional exercises for use with Section D, Review Unit 4, Part 2

1 Listen to the third verse and correct any mistakes in the version below:

I have slipped on a Yankee slipper chip
Davy Crockett is her fame.
Sand her Captain's game it is Burgess,
Hand they lay she's a boating lane.

2 Now listen to verses 4 and 5 and say whether the following statements are true or false:

a The tug is waiting at the mouth of the river.
b The ship's sails are unfurled.
c The anchor is still down.
d The singer will be away from Liverpool for a considerable period.